YANKEE ADMIRAL

A biography of David Dixon Porter, the Civil War hero who was the father of the modern Navy

Noel B. Gerson

SAPERE
BOOKS

For
Louis P. Saxe

YANKEE
ADMIRAL

Published by Sapere Books.

20 Windermere Drive, Leeds, England, LS17 7UZ,
United Kingdom

saperebooks.com

ISBN: 978-1-80055-099-5.

My honor, my country, my family — and, always, the Navy. They are my life, one and inseparable.
David Dixon Porter, Admiral, United States Navy

Table of Contents

I

COMMODORE DAVID PORTER took it for granted that his sons would follow him into the United States Navy, and whatever the gifted, hot-tempered, courageous, and quarrelsome hero assumed Evalina Anderson Porter accepted with patient resignation. So the future of David Dixon Porter, their second son, was settled the day of his birth, June 8, 1813, at the comfortable family home near Chester, Pennsylvania.

Neither they nor anyone else, however, could have predicted that he would rise to heights never before scaled by an American seaman, or that his renown would eclipse his father's. Porter's foster-brother, David Glasgow Farragut, the nation's first admiral, in whose footsteps he would follow, said of him, "In battle or war council, planning for the future or utilizing the resources at hand, I would rather have him at my side than any man I know."

President Ulysses S. Grant, who had known David as a comrade in arms and as a subordinate, went a step farther when he declared, "Porter is as great an admiral as Horatio Nelson."

David Dixon Porter lived in a sophisticated age of steam as well as of sail, so it may be that the comparison was not valid, but comparisons are irrelevant. He was a superb sailor and fighting man, a renowned scientist, a distinguished educator, and, on occasion, a reckless, hot-headed daredevil. It is difficult to measure the enormity of his contributions to both the science and the strategic concepts of modern naval warfare. He came of age with steam, and moved into a position of high command with a ship that was unique — the ironclad.

It was he who first utilized the concept of massed naval firepower in offensive operations. He was the first to demonstrate the relative invulnerability of the "metal warship" in conducting defense operations. His inventions, including new torpedoes and other mechanical devices, changed the basic nature of naval warfare, bringing about the first great revolution at sea since the time of the ancient Phoenicians. And, although he died in 1891, his influence is felt down to the present day in the United States Navy and other navies, thanks to the many farsighted changes he introduced into the educational system at the U.S. Naval Academy.

Perhaps it might be argued that the coming of steam and the "metal ship" made inevitable many of the ideas that David Dixon Porter initiated, developed, and demonstrated. Such a claim, however, would be meaningless and patently unfair to a man who literally brought a new dimension to naval warfare. Porter was a genius, an innovator courageous enough to put his dreams to the ultimate test and prove their worth. Every American is in his debt, as are the citizens of all seagoing nations.

United States Congressman William Anderson had served in the Revolutionary War as a major, and his daughter, Evalina, knew nothing about the sea when she married Captain David Porter of the new Navy. But, settling down with him in the house on a hill overlooking the Delaware River near Chester, Pennsylvania, that her father had given them as a wedding present, she learned quickly. David was a devoted husband and equally devoted father to the four sons and one daughter born to them by 1819, but the sea was ever-present in his mind, and, as he himself said, in his blood.

The hot-tempered veteran of the young nation's undeclared war with the Barbary pirates of North Africa was given command of the thirty-two-gun frigate, *Essex*, when the War of 1812 broke out, and went off to sea in the autumn of that year, leaving his wife and their three-year-old son, William, at Chester. When he returned home two years later, a national hero, with the exploits of the *Essex* already legendary, his second son, David Dixon, was fifteen months old.

According to legend, the fierce, bearded officer threw the baby high in the air, tweaked his eagle-like nose and large ears, so similar to his own, and unleashed a string of seafarer's oaths so violently colorful that his wife and the servants fled from the nursery. He later boasted to friends that the baby, laughing equally hard, pulled his own nose in return. The gesture was prophetic: David Dixon never allowed anyone — not even the father he came to revere and respect above all men — to strike at him without retaliating in kind.

When the war ended, Captain Porter was promoted to the rank of commodore, then the highest in the Navy, and with two colleagues, Stephen Decatur and John Rodgers, was assigned to the Board of Navy Commissioners. In other words, he and his peers became the uniformed heads of the Navy. Many years later the posts were combined in the single office of Chief of Naval Operations. The commodore bought a new house in Washington which was then a raw, uncompleted city of dirt roads and unpainted buildings. His home, however, was elegant, civilized, and comfortable, though his family did not move in until it was completely ready for occupancy, in 1819.

By that time David Dixon was six years old. In addition to William, there were three other children: Elizabeth, Thomas, and the new infant, Theodoric. All of them, with the exception of David Dixon, were well-behaved, but his pranks made up for the obedience of the others. Less than a month after the family moved into the new house, the little boy was discovered by the servants on the lawn, peering through the prized spyglass that his father had carried on board the *Essex*.

The children had been forbidden to touch any of the commodore's seagoing belongings, but when David was taken before his mother, he offered no excuse. He had wanted to see the President's house, which had been painted white to hide the scars inflicted on it when the British had burned it during the war, so he had "borrowed" the glass. A spanking did not prevent the boy from taking the glass on two other occasions.

Lieutenant David Farragut, who had been adopted by the commodore as a child and had gone to sea with him on the *Essex*, came to the house with his bride for a long visit, and David Dixon began his relationship with the officer, then in his twenties, with whom he would be so closely associated during his career. The solemn young man and the mischievous little boy immediately established a rapport that lasted as long as they lived.

Farragut took young David with him to a concert of the Marine Band, the pride of the Navy; and David, sneaking away from his escort, joined the band in its parade to the White House lawn. Commodore Porter was not amused, but Farragut's intervention saved the child from the most dreaded of all punishment — a spanking by his father.

One event that took place in 1819 — his formal introduction to the Navy — remained vividly in David Dixon's memory until the end of his days. He had grown accustomed to the presence of blue-clad officers at his parents' dinner table, of course, but he had witnessed no Navy ceremonies. The commodore remedied that deficiency by taking his three eldest children to the commissioning of the new forty-four-gun ship-of-the-line, the *Columbus*, at the Navy Yard on the Potomac River.

The boy was awed by his father's full-dress uniform and that of Farragut, who acted as the commodore's aide-de-camp. The crashing of cannon left an indelible impression on David, as did the presentation of the *Columbus'* flag to her captain by the commissioners, and the subsequent establishment of the ship's watch. For days afterward David and his brother, William, wearing toy swords that Farragut had given them, marched up and down the decks of an imaginary ship in the Porter yard. William sometimes became bored by the game, but David was tireless, and even when his brother went elsewhere to play, remained "on watch."

The Navy Yard became a second home to David, who was allowed to roam through the place at will whenever he could persuade his father to take him there. He climbed into sentry boxes, watched workmen building new ships, and occasionally "helped" them, pounding a nail into an oak plank, or sawing off a jagged end. He also learned about his father's ordeal during the Barbary War when, as first lieutenant of the captured frigate, *Philadelphia*, he had spent many months as a prisoner in Tripoli.

Sailors who had been members of the ship's crew told him something of that ugly experience. Most of the details, however, were filled in by Commodore William Bainbridge, who had been the *Philadelphia*'s captain. From his father's former superior and lifelong friend the boy gained an appreciation of the heroism and courage that his father — always reticent about his own exploits — never mentioned.

Other visitors to the Porter home included the Navy's great men — Stephen Decatur, John Rodgers, and Oliver H. Perry, as well as Bainbridge. All of them were obliged to talk of the sea to a boy who never tired of listening, or of asking countless questions. "David Dixon," Commodore Rodgers once said, "fell in love with the sea before he'd put out in anything bigger than a rowing boat!"

The source of most stories was the man closest to the child, his father, who illustrated his tales of adventure on the high seas by showing the wide-eyed David his trophies — among them, razor-sharp cutlasses, barbed harpoons, and dueling pistols with hair-triggers. On several occasions the boy was treated to unexpected fireworks when the commodore and Decatur, both of them explosive, became involved in violent arguments over the past, and turned the air blue with their language.

By the time David Dixon was nine, he could curse as fluently as any man who had spent a life at sea, but he had to be careful not to show off his knowledge in the presence of adults. His mother had washed out his mouth with soft, yellow soap on the one occasion when she had heard him, and he shuddered to think of how his father might react.

In that same year, 1822, an incident occurred that the boy never forgot, and with good reason. His father's prized pets were a flock of Barbary pigeons, which had been pampered since his enforced stay in Tripoli. They and their descendants filled the many cages of a pigeon house built for them on the grounds of the Washington mansion, and every visitor was invited to inspect them. David, who had been learning to use firearms, saw the birds not as prized exhibits of a species unknown in the New World, but as natural targets for a boy anxious to try out the double-barreled rifle hanging above the hearth in his father's library.

Certainly he knew what would happen to him if he used the rifle without permission, to say nothing of shooting at the pigeons, but the temptation nagged at him, and one sunny spring afternoon his chance came. His mother and the English nurse were occupied in the nursery with the new baby, Hambleton; the commodore was working at his office; and the servants were busy in other parts of the house. It was easy for the boy to take the rifle from its place above the mantel, collect bullets and gunpowder from a drawer in his father's unlocked desk, and wander out into the yard.

The shutters of the pigeon house were open, and the fluttering, squawking birds proved to be an irresistible lure. David loaded the rifle, carefully observing the safety rules he had been taught. After a moment, several shots shattered the quiet of the warm afternoon.

By the time a small army of servants reached the yard, some thirty shots had been fired, and the high-powered bullets had killed at least a score of birds. David, who had been fascinated by his own prowess and had been staring at the cages, suddenly realized it would be prudent to take himself elsewhere. Still carrying the rifle, he ran to the rear of the stable, but quickly decided the refuge was too close to the house, and slipped off into the adjoining orchard where he tried to hide behind a cherry tree.

At best he could not have hoped to escape unpunished, but on that particular day his luck deserted him completely. The commodore, suffering from an unaccustomed headache, and in a bad temper, arrived home unexpectedly while the furor was at its height. The situation was explained to him, and after a grim survey of the slaughtered birds, he started toward the garden.

Trapped, with no place to go, David climbed up into the cherry tree, still carrying the rifle. Waiting there in tense, uneasy silence, the squeaking of the garden gate heralding the approach of the commodore sounded to him like the crack of doom.

The boy thought himself invisible, but his father, ominously swishing his riding crop, came to the foot of the cherry tree and ordered him to come down. David Dixon obeyed, laid the rifle at his father's feet, and then was given the thrashing of his life. He could not sit in comfort for several days, but the worst of the experience, he later recalled, was that his father did not say a single word to him. The punishment was administered in an ominous silence that was far worse than the thrashing.

A week later Commodore Porter summoned his son to the library, and astonished the boy by offering him a half-interest in the surviving pigeons. There was only one condition: David would be required to take care of the birds.

"My father could have found no better way to curb and discipline a rebellious boy," he wrote many years later.

Significant events changed David Dixon's life when he was ten and eleven years old. The first occurred on January 1, 1823, when William Porter received a warrant as a midshipman in the Navy, and his young brother enviously watched him go off to sea. David was not only deprived of his constant playmate's company, but suddenly recognized the jelling of his own goals: he, too, wanted to work for a commission at the first opportunity.

Meanwhile, the commodore found himself in financial difficulty. His family was still growing and his estate was costing him a small fortune to operate. Accordingly, he applied for sea duty, where he would earn more than he could on land. Specifically, he requested permission to rid the Caribbean Sea of the pirates who were preying on the merchant ships of all nations trading in the tropical islands.

The situation in the West Indies was delicate. Mexico, Venezuela, and Santo Domingo had declared themselves independent of Spain, and the Spanish government had retaliated by blockading their coasts. Buccaneers — bold seafaring men from all parts of the world — came to the Caribbean to help the rebels. The governments of the infant, self-proclaimed republics could not afford to pay their "volunteer helpers," who quickly turned to piracy as a means of making their living.

The problem was complicated by the venality of Spanish officials stationed in Cuba and other colonies of Madrid. It was known in Washington that Spaniards of the highest rank in the New World were accepting bribes from the pirates, and conveniently looking the other way when American and other merchant ships were captured and looted. The United States was anxious to avoid any unpleasantness with Spain that might give Madrid the excuse to regain lost prestige by declaring war on the young, still struggling North American nation. So Commodore Porter was directed to do nothing that might offend Spain when he put out to sea.

To the relief of Navy colleagues who knew Commodore Porter's bold, impetuous nature, he conducted himself with such circumspection in his campaign of 1823 that he not only made an effective beginning in his attempt to rid the Caribbean of pirates, but did nothing that caused Spanish officials to complain. The Navy Department increased the commodore's squadron for the 1824 campaign, and allowed him to take his family with him on board his flagship, the frigate *John Adams*.

Thus, on December 10, 1823, David Dixon went to sea for the first time, and spent all of his waking hours on deck, watching officers and seamen, listening, and asking endless questions. Five days later the flagship anchored off Norfolk,

Virginia. Here the boy became acquainted with the schooners under his father's command — the *Grampus*, the *Weazle*, the *Spark*, and the *Sea Gull*. He went on board — all of them, but it was the *Sea Gull* that absorbed his interest. A one-time ferry boat that had been converted into a steamship, she was clumsy, slow, and cramped; nevertheless, she had the distinction of being the first steamer ever to be commissioned as a warship. David spent several days aboard the *Sea Gull*, avidly learning every detail of her operation.

The commodore, delayed because he had to testify before a court-martial board, quietly ordered his officers to treat David like a midshipman, and the boy was subjected to a rigorous training. He responded enthusiastically, soon was able to climb high in the rigging of the *John Adams*, even in rough seas, and was taught the rudiments of every sailor's routine.

On February 18th, the squadron finally put to sea, and from then until mid-May the boy gained practical experience under sailing conditions, displaying such quick agility and such instinctive understanding of the sea's many moods that his father was delighted. The future was settled: David Dixon would become an officer in the Navy.

The idyll ended abruptly when the commodore fell ill, forcing the cancellation of the cruise and making it necessary for Mrs. Porter to return to Washington with her five children. David came back to solid earth — literally — and instead of enjoying life on the high seas, was sent to boarding school. He had to remind himself that he was growing too old to cry, but it wasn't easy to control his tears of disappointment.

Columbia College, actually a preparatory school, was located only a short distance from the Porter mansion, but young Porter lived in the school dormitory with the other ninety-two students. His studies included the usual nineteenth century subjects — English and the classics, Latin and Greek, and mathematics. He worked diligently in his mathematics classes, which were essential to any future navigation officer. Sometimes, he confessed in later years, he applied himself less vigorously to his studies of subjects that, in his opinion, would not mean much in a Navy life.

In all, he spent two years at the school. Meanwhile, his father became involved in a sensational incident. A young Navy officer, who had gone ashore at the town of Fajardo in Spanish Puerto Rico had been insulted by the mayor and other authorities. Commodore Porter had promptly landed there himself, taking a large company of seamen with him, and had forced the Spaniards to make an abject apology which he had dictated to them at gunpoint, word for word.

The affair created an uproar in Washington. Less than a year earlier, President James Monroe had issued the Monroe Doctrine, prepared by Secretary of State John Quincy Adams, warning Europe not to commit aggression or interfere in the politics of any Western Hemisphere nations. As interpreted at the time, the Doctrine implied that the United States would not disturb the status quo in any New World colonies of European powers.

Therefore, the Administration had good cause to fear that the United States had given Spain an excuse to declare war. The President and Adams were alarmed, and Secretary of the Navy, Samuel Southard, recalled Commodore Porter to Washington to explain the affair. Before he arrived, Administration strategists decided to establish a board of inquiry to investigate the incident.

The idea made sense. If Spain was in a belligerent mood, the inquiry would indicate that Washington was taking an impartial stand, and that Porter was not necessarily being supported. On the other hand, the commodore would not necessarily be condemned for having done his duty as he had seen fit.

The fiery veteran believed that his Government was trying to make him a scapegoat, however, and arrived in Washington, early in the spring of 1825, in a violently angry frame of mind. To the surprise of the Administration, Spain had not protested the affair, so the hearings of the board were postponed. Had the commodore remained silent, nothing more would have happened, and he would have been returned to sea duty.

But two New England Congressmen and several newspapers in the area attacked him, and he ignored the advice of friends who pointed out to him that the sentiments of the region had not changed since, a decade earlier, it had strongly opposed the War of 1812. Insisting that his honor was at stake, he wrote an intemperate letter to Southard, demanding that the board meet in the near future, and that he either be cleared or dismissed from the Navy.

The astonished secretary had little choice left, and after writing Porter, to reprimand him for the language he had used, he summoned the board to meet early in May. The commodore's anger was further aroused when he learned that Commodore James Barron would be a member of the board. He himself had served on a court-martial board that had tried Barron in 1807, and because his own vote had gone against the defendant, he now believed that the Navy Department had deliberately selected someone antagonistic to him for the task of investigating his own conduct.

Fireworks erupted on the opening day of the hearings when Commodore Porter was asked whether he objected to anyone's participating in the inquiry. In his mind the real villain was Secretary Southard, and he made a speech highly uncomplimentary to the character and motives of the Navy Department's civilian head.

The courtroom was cleared; Porter's remarks were found objectionable; and he was asked to retract the more violent of them. He not only refused, but stalked out of the room, and the inquiry was forced to proceed without him. He defended himself by writing a pamphlet, in which his language was even stronger, and dedicated the document — which he published at his own expense — to the new President, John Quincy Adams.

Southard had been vilified to an extent that he could not ignore and so ordered the commodore to be court-martialed. The trial was a sensation. The aroused Porter attended only a few of its sessions, spending the better part of his time launching new, furious attacks on Southard. He refused to listen to the friends who repeatedly told him that he was doing incalculable harm to his own cause.

The verdict of the court was remarkably lenient. Commodore Porter was suspended from active duty for a period of six months, but the court made it clear that the suspension was in no way to prejudice his future service in the Navy. In addition, he was completely exonerated for his conduct in Puerto Rico, the court declaring that he had maintained the honor and advanced the interests of his nation and her Navy.

Commodore Porter, however, was unable to see the judgment in a reasonable light. He had been disgraced forever by personal enemies, he declared, and retired to his mansion to brood in silence for the six-months' period of his suspension.

David Dixon, at the age of thirteen, was horrified by the catastrophe. He was convinced that his father was the most perfect of men, incapable of doing wrong, a belief he held for the rest of his life. The commodore's enemies became young David's enemies, and he swore vengeance against them. Later, during his Navy career, he was destined to serve under four different members of the court-martial board, and at no time did he deal with them in the respectful manner befitting a young officer.

As aggressive and determined as his father, with the same deep love of the sea, and, at times, the same hot temper, he became obsessed with the idea of restoring the honor of the Porter name. In order to understand his career, it is necessary to remember that, no matter how great his achievements, he never thought them sufficient. Other, higher goals always loomed above him, and he worked furiously to attain them.

The court-martial had another lasting effect on David Dixon. He felt a loathing for all politicians, and to the end of his life treated them with open contempt. In view of the obstacles that he himself created, it is astonishing that he succeeded in rising so high in his country's service.

His renown, however, lay far in the future. All he knew was that he felt utterly crushed when, in the spring of 1826, his father resigned from the United States Navy on the day his six-month's suspension ended. The heartbroken boy returned home from school, dazed by the tragedy.

He had no way of knowing that a man of his father's disposition could not remain inactive, and that his immediate plans included an exciting and adventurous career for his second and favorite son.

II

FORMER Commodore Porter stunned his many loyal friends and equally numerous foes in the spring of 1826 by accepting an appointment as commander in chief of the Mexican Navy, with the rank of General of Marine. American newspapers published long editorials on the subject, some debating the propriety of a former high-ranking United States officer transferring his allegiance to an alien power. Neither the disturbed editors nor the overwrought members of the United States Senate and House of Representatives, who raised the subject in Congress, realized that the commodore still considered himself an American. He had taken a high post under the flag of a foreign nation, but remained loyal to his native land.

It is not known how Mrs. Porter, who remained behind in Washington, reacted to her husband's startling decision. She had had her hands full taking care of Elizabeth, Theodoric, Hambleton, and her new-born twins, Henry and Evalina.

Only two Americans rejoiced. David Dixon Porter and his younger brother, Thomas, accompanied their father and were enrolled as midshipmen in the Mexican Navy. The party sailed for Mexico from New York in the late spring of 1826 on board the frigate, *Guerrero*, commanded by the general of marine's twenty-one-year-old nephew, D. Henry Porter, who had resigned his commission as a lieutenant in the United States Navy in order to serve under him. So David Dixon's first captain was his cousin, and on the voyage to Vera Cruz he also remained under the stern, ever-critical eye of his father.

Life aboard the frigate was strenuous, but the *Guerrero* cast anchor at Vera Cruz in early June, and David suffered another disappointment when he and Thomas were sent to boarding school in Mexico City for seven months while their father tried to create a fighting force out of old, creaking ships the new Republic of Mexico had purchased from other nations.

There were other, frustrating delays while the general of marine tried to create a disciplined force of officers and men, and David did not go to sea until the early summer of 1827. He was assigned a berth on his father's flagship, the frigate *Libertade*, and spent every evening in his father's cabin, receiving priceless personal instruction. He was taught navigation and gunnery, the principles and techniques of command, and, above all, the rudiments of discipline.

He was an eager pupil, and by autumn his father decided he was ready for the next step in his education-life at sea under combat conditions. Accordingly, he was transferred to the *Esmeralda*, a merchantman that had been converted into a brig-of-war, commanded by his cousin, Henry. D. Henry Porter was ordered to harass Spanish shipping in the vicinity of Cuba, and he met with considerable initial success, capturing and sinking four heavily-laden merchant vessels. But his undisciplined crew mutinied, so — aided by his two American officers and young cousin — he was compelled to use force in order to restore order.

The captain and his first lieutenant killed two seamen, put the other mutineers in irons and sailed back to Vera Cruz. David's role was that of an observer, but he learned a lesson he would never forget. As his father had told him many times, a ship's master was the sole, unquestioned ruler of his floating domain, and would lose control of his vessel if he allowed even the slightest deviation from his orders. The boy, who had seen blood spilled for the first time, was beginning to grow up.

Early in 1828, the *Guerrero* was dispatched on a mission similar to that of the *Esmeralda*. Again D. Henry Porter was in command, with an Englishman named Williams as his first lieutenant, two American lieutenants, and a crew that was one-third Mexican and two-thirds American and English. David and several other American boys sailed as midshipmen, attending classes, serving as apprentice officers, and working for sixteen hours out of every twenty-four.

Soon after the *Guerrero* arrived off the coast of Cuba on February 10th, the lookout in the crow's nest spotted a number of merchant schooners, escorted by two Spanish brigs-of-war, the *Amalia* and *Marte*. Captain D. Henry Porter tacked, ordered his frigate stripped for action, and moved in for the kill. The Spanish convoy fled toward the little port of Mariel, about thirty miles west of Havana, which was protected by a stone fortress tower equipped with two long guns.

The battle was soon intensified, with the American and English gunners on the *Guerrero* sinking several of the enemy merchantmen and crippling the *Amalia* so badly that she, too, sought refuge in Mariel. But the attacker, fighting against heavy odds, did not escape unscathed. Her cable was severed, which caused her to drift; both of her topgallant masts were shot away, and her rigging was slashed repeatedly. Her casualties were light, however. Only ten to fifteen members of her crew were killed or wounded; the exact number was never determined.

In any event, Captain D. Henry Porter still had the strength and capability of finishing what he had started. The fire from the fort was inaccurate, and only the *Marte* still stood between him and the surviving merchantmen. So he gave the order to sail still closer to shore.

David Dixon was enjoying every moment of his first battle. He raced from one end of the ship to the other, carrying the orders of the captain to subordinates, and not even the sight of the dead and wounded disturbed him. Years later he revealed that a spent cannon ball had struck him on the leg, leaving a bruise, but his exhilaration at the moment was so great that he did not feel the impact.

Victory was in the air, and the captain thought it likely that he could force the enemy to surrender before nightfall. But the fortunes of war changed quickly. The sound of gunfire had been heard near Havana, and the sixty-four-gun ship-of-the-line *Lealtad*, flagship of the Spanish fleet in the Caribbean, bore down on the *Guerrero* under full sail.

Captain D. Henry Porter realized, of course, that his twenty-two-gun frigate was no match for the larger vessel, and, abandoning his attack, put out to sea in an attempt to escape. Even though he was sailing a crippled ship, his superior seamanship prevailed. He tacked frequently, and, although his guns had a shorter range than those of the *Lealtad*, his fire was more accurate, and his destruction of the Spaniard's foremast enabled him to get away.

A prudent master would have left the scene, thankful for the cover of night, but the captain was young — and a hot-blooded Porter besides. He summoned his officers to a council of war, and they endorsed the bold scheme he outlined to them. He told them the Spaniards undoubtedly believed the *Guerrero* had sailed away, and were probably relaxing their vigilance. He therefore proposed that the frigate turn back, complete her destruction of the merchantmen and the *Marte*, and then sail away again before daybreak.

David Dixon had no voice in the matter, but he enthusiastically agreed with his cousin's plan. "I was too young," he wrote many years later, "to recognize the risks we were taking, and too inexperienced to know what needed to be done in order to overcome them."

The captain of the *Lealtad* proved to be less lethargic than the Americans had assumed, and soon after she tacked, her decks were raked by a concentrated broadside. The *Guerrero's* mainmast was shattered, making it impossible for her to sail at a pace faster than a crawl, but she tried valiantly to escape.

Her efforts were fruitless. The *Lealtad* crossed back and forth across her path, systematically destroying her, and by dawn she was little better than a hulk. Twice her colors had been shot away and twice replaced, but a short time after the sun rose, Captain D. Henry Porter knew he was beaten. Again he called a conference on his quarterdeck, and his officers agreed that he should surrender.

He hauled down his colors, though the Spaniards later explained they believed they had shot down the ensign. Still firing broadsides, they switched to "grape" when they reached short range. Small, deadly chunks of metal rained down on the helpless *Guerrero*, killing and wounding forty percent of the frigate's men. The captain was struck in the head and stomach, and died a moment later in the arms of his young cousin. And David Dixon was beginning to understand the horrors of war.

The boy was wildly angry, and for the rest of his life condemned the callous brutality of a foe who had, he believed, violated the code of honor traditionally observed in war at sea. His hatred became even more intense when boarding parties from the *Lealtad* arrived to make the survivors their prisoners, and he saw the lifeless body of his cousin being thrown overboard.

When the captives reached Havana and the Spanish authorities there learned David Dixon's identity, they immediately offered the young midshipman the gentleman's parole customarily granted an officer. This meant that he could take up residence in a comfortable Havana inn, dine where he pleased, amuse himself in any manner he saw fit, and enjoy himself while he waited for his father to arrange an exchange of prisoners.

But young Porter's fury was so great that he unhesitatingly rejected the offer, electing instead to accompany the other members of the *Guerrero's* crew to a prison ship in the harbor. There he spent six months under living conditions more primitive and barbaric than he had ever imagined possible.

The prisoners were confined in dark, damp quarters below decks. Not once during the six months of their incarceration were they permitted to go into the open for fresh air and sunlight. The summer heat was stifling; the ship was infested with insects and rats; and thirty-one of the ninety-two captives died. Sanitary facilities were virtually non-existent, and the prisoners could neither obtain clean clothes nor wash the filthy rags they wore.

The worst of their misery was the slop they were served in the guise of food. Their meals consisted of two slices of stale bread and two bowls of watery soup each day, and in the first weeks of their imprisonment the starving men were almost reduced to the point of attacking their fellows in order to obtain a larger share of the rations.

Porter became a member of a self-appointed group that maintained order, prevented theft, and stopped fights before they began. Although only fifteen, he conducted himself with the self-control of a man twice his age, and under the most trying circumstances never lost his dignity.

"He remembered, at all times, that he was a Porter," a fellow American midshipman, Andrew Bruce, later wrote. "We who had known the commodore sometimes thought it was he who exhorted and scolded us, lost his temper with us when we quarreled, and displayed the most tender-hearted solicitude when our spirits sank so low that we sat on the rotting decks and wept."

The men of the Porter family were tall, although not particularly sturdy or heavily built, and it is surprising that David Dixon suffered no permanent ill effects. But his long imprisonment neither hindered his growth nor scarred his soul. He, like his companions, thought it likely that the entire company would die before an exchange of prisoners could be worked out with the Mexicans. In fact, having seen Spanish cruelty at close range, he believed it probable that the authorities in Havana had announced to the world that no one on board the *Guerrero* had survived the battle with the *Lealtad*.

He had already developed inner resources that enabled him to remain cheerful, however. Bruce said that he had never heard young Porter complain about their miserable existence. Only when a companion mentioned the Spaniards did he lose his self-control, and on several occasions some of the older men were forced to restrain him when he wanted to make his way to the quarters of the prison ship's officers and kill them.

What he did not know was that a list of the survivors had been sent to Mexico City, and that General of Marine Porter had received a courteous offer from the Spanish Admiralty Board in Havana to set his son free as a token of their good faith before opening negotiations for an exchange of other prisoners. Surely the elder Porter was tempted, but he placed duty and honor above all other considerations. He wanted no favors, he replied, and sought the release of all survivors of the *Guerrero* — not just one.

The negotiations were interminable, the difficulty of communicating between Havana and Mexico City making them even longer, and not until August 8th, almost a full six months after they had been captured, were the men on the prison ship released. A large crowd had gathered on shore to watch the event, and when the prisoners straggled up into the unaccustomed sunlight, young Porter assigned his companions to military ranks and marched them across the deck to the boats that waited to take them ashore.

The master of an American merchantman was waiting for Porter with a letter and a purse from his father. The message was crisp, almost impersonal, but the boy read between the lines and his heart ached for his proud father. The house in Washington had been sold at a fraction of what it had cost, and the family had moved back to Chester, Pennsylvania. The former commodore, desperately in need of the wages he earned and his share of the prize money he won when Spanish ships fell into Mexican hands, was keeping his position as general of marine. He directed his son to return home, however, because his mother needed him.

Whether Porter wanted to rejoin his father, or sail on another Mexican warship, he did not express his desires to anyone. He had been given an order by the man whose word was law to him, and he unhesitatingly obeyed it.

He learned that the merchant ship would give him passage to New Orleans, but he brusquely rejected the offer that he spend several days in Havana, recuperating from his ordeal and buying new clothes. He insisted that he would spend no time on Spanish soil, and was rowed out to the merchantman, still clad in his prison rags.

Once he reached the American ship he stripped, and with a sailor pumping up water from the bay, used a hose to give himself his first bath in months. He spent more than an hour under the hose, used two full cups of soft soap and scrubbed himself until his skin was raw. His filthy prison attire having been burned, he bought clothing from the junior officers and crew members, and at last considered himself fit company for his fellow countrymen.

Then, adjourning to the cramped cabin the officers used as a wardroom, he sat down to an enormous meal of soup and bread, two kinds of fish and three kinds of meat. He was warned against overeating after barely existing for so many months on a stringent diet, but he ignored the advice — and suffered no ill effects. Then he adjourned to the cabin of the two junior mates, where a hammock had been strung for him, and for the first time in six months slept soundly — a luxury after having had only dirty planks for a bed.

For the next four days, while the brig remained anchored in Havana's harbor, taking on cargo, Porter did little except take two baths daily, eat, and sleep. The change in his appearance was immediate. He rapidly regained much of the weight he had lost, and recovered the store of seemingly inexhaustible energy that all Porters possessed.

On the voyage to New Orleans he continued to eat heartily, to sleep long hours, and bathe frequently. But his interest in sailing was so intense that, with the master's permission, he also spent several hours on the quarterdeck each day, absorbing all he could learn about navigation, the wind, and the sea.

One afternoon an intense "whirlwind gale" struck the brig — the type of storm that later would become known as a hurricane. Fascinated by the turbulence, Porter remained on the quarterdeck for the better part of the forty-eight hours that the ship fought its way in the storm. This was his first recorded experience at sea in such weather, and he was interested in gaining first-hand experience in dealing with such a situation. Nothing is known of what contribution he may have made to the operation of the vessel during the storm, but it is unlikely that he remained a mere observer. His own nature would have prevented him from being idle, and in a hurricane all hands were needed, so it is probable that the master took advantage of his presence to press him into service.

By the time the brig arrived in New Orleans Porter no longer showed any effects of his imprisonment. He had gained so much weight that the clothes he had bought from the crew members had grown tight, and he had to dip into the purse his father had sent him to buy still another wardrobe.

Porter remained in New Orleans for about a week, seeing the sights of the town, and, in particular, visiting the battlefield where General Andrew Jackson, now President of the United States, had defeated a corps of British Regulars in the climactic battle of the War of 1812. He continued to eat ravenously and sleep long hours. He also discovered that girls were staring at him, nudging one another and giggling, when he walked past them in the streets.

Already six feet tall, he had developed a thicker chest than other members of his family. His dark eyes were mischievous and lively, but his imprisonment had given him an intensity of expression unusual in one so young. His dark, straight hair was neatly combed, his sharp nose and firm jaw showed his strength of character, and his erect bearing, which soon would be called "arrogant," further singled him out for attention. He was surprised to find that he was returning the interest of the girls; until now his one passion in life had been the sea, and it disturbed him to think that there might be distracting influences in the years to come.

One unusual facet of Porter's nature that had become more and more evident was his photographic memory. He found he could remember, at will, anything he saw or read. The unusual gift of total recall would be of extraordinary value, almost thirty-five years later, when he played a major role in Admiral Farragut's capture of New Orleans in the Civil War.

Porter's stay in New Orleans was marred by sad news that arrived in a brief note written to him by his father. His brother, Thomas, had died unexpectedly of yellow fever in Vera Cruz. Knowing that his mother would need him more than ever now, he arranged for his passage home, paying for transportation by boat as far as Pittsburgh, and for a stagecoach seat to Philadelphia from that city.

He had recovered his natural buoyancy by the time he sailed north on a Mississippi River steamer, and on the trip suffered a humiliation he would never forget. Two professional gamblers were passengers on the ship, and persuaded him to play a "friendly" game of cards with them. Porter promptly lost his entire purse, except for the sum he had kept in reserve to cover his expenses on the rest of the voyage.

The gamblers left the ship at Vicksburg, and the incident was closed, but during the Civil War, when he was subjecting that city to an intense bombardment of thirteen-inch mortar shells, he would recall them, and wonder what had become of them.

The hours that Porter spent with the river pilot in the wheelhouse of the little steamer proved to be of incalculable value to him, a generation later. He learned that Mississippi River navigation was unique, presenting problems unknown on any other North American waterway. The channel shifted constantly, as did the speed of the current as the river flowed southward to the Gulf of Mexico. Even in its deepest portions the channel was shallow, and there was an ever-present danger of going aground on submerged sandbars — or, more properly, bars of mud. Pilots also had to remain on guard against the further hazard of striking sharp, hidden rocks that could damage the hulls of even the strongest ships.

Particularly interesting and disturbing to Porter was the fact that it was almost impossible for an outsider, even a veteran navigator, to detect these obstacles. Only a man who sailed up and down the Mississippi constantly, season after season, year after year, and was familiar with the river and the terrain of its banks could consider himself capable of piloting a ship through its treacherous waters. It is small wonder that, in his expeditions on the Mississippi during the Civil War, Porter always took the precaution of hiring at least one, and preferably two, civilian pilots to guide his flotilla from his lead ship.

The voyage was leisurely, and with time on his hands, Porter spent long hours reminiscing about all the things that had happened to him since he had accompanied his father to Mexico on the ill-fated *Guerrero*. It was natural that he should dwell on the climax of his months abroad, especially the battle off the coast of Cuba, and he pondered the question of what might have been done to turn defeat into victory.

Analyzing every detail of what had happened in the fight with the *Lealtad*, he finally reached the conclusion that his cousin had erred in trying to escape from the larger, more powerful ship. The American and English gunners on board the *Guerrero* had been far superior to the Spanish gunners, and if the Mexican frigate had sailed as closely as possible to the ship-of-the-line, firing steadily at point-blank range, the battle might have been won.

As he imagined the situation, the *Guerrero* might have been able to inflict heavy damage on her foe while suffering relatively light punishment herself, particularly if the frigate's gunners had first concentrated on knocking out the larger ship's cannon. Then, thanks to her superior speed and maneuverability, the *Guerrero* could have escaped, leaving her opponent a battered hulk.

In essence, Porter decided, his cousin had made the mistake of trying to flee from a stronger force instead of realizing that his gunnery gave him the advantage. Attack was the best of all possible tactics, and was most likely to guarantee success in battle. Even when the odds favored a foe, a vigorous attack was preferable to evasion or retreat, and if pressed boldly, could be counted on to disconcert an enemy.

What was remarkable about Porter's thinking was the fact that he was still an adolescent in his mid-teens. The concept of relying consistently on attack would become an essential aspect of the principle of naval warfare that he later developed, and at no time in his life did he alter this philosophy. Equally astonishing is that the idea was his own. To some extent he was indebted to the greatest of British admirals, but not even Horatio Nelson had advocated the pressing of an attack under any and all circumstances, no matter what the odds were against a force. To be sure, Nelson favored the bold attack, but he always assumed that an assault force would be sufficiently powerful to assure success.

Porter was even more audacious than the brilliant Englishman. Like Nelson, he knew that the element of chance was always present in battle, and that the human reactions to stress played a vital role in determining the outcome. His theory was predicated on the realization, always emphasized by his father, that it was impossible to give officers and seamen enough disciplined training for war. When cannon were fired and shot fell, men became fearful, panicky, and illogical. Therefore, he reasoned, the side that pressed the attack gained an advantage, even when it was outnumbered.

His debt to his father was obvious. He could not have formulated his tactics had he not listened, since earliest childhood, to stories of experiences accumulated over a lifetime at sea. How much he consciously owed Admiral Nelson cannot be measured so easily. Every high-ranking officer in the United States Navy admired Nelson, and was thoroughly acquainted with his strategy and tactics. There were books and charts of his engagements in the family library, and Porter, late in life, once remarked that he had studied the Battles of the Nile and Trafalgar soon after he had first learned to read.

Therefore, Horatio Nelson must share the credit with Commodore Porter for providing the background that enabled David Dixon to create a new approach to war at sea. A youngster who had fought in only one engagement lacked the wisdom to grasp broad principles, but the fact remains that Porter did understand what experienced officers three times his age could not envisage. He was a genius in naval matters, which partly explains his ability to formulate a new doctrine. But he also enjoyed unique advantages. Not only was he a pupil of Commodore Porter, but he learned from such officers as Decatur and Bainbridge and Rodgers. The education he acquired was as priceless as the doctrines he evolved.

In any event, Porter's homeward journey was placid after the gamblers disembarked at Vicksburg, and he arrived at Chester in mid-autumn. His brothers and sisters were delighted to see him, and gave him a hero's welcome. His mother greeted him warmly, and at once enrolled him in the Chester Academy for Young Men.

The war veteran, who had spent six months as a prisoner of the Spaniards, glumly returned to his studies of the classics, ancient languages, and mathematics. What he did not know was that his days as a civilian were numbered.

III

EARLY in January, 1829, Congressman William Anderson submitted a petition to the Navy Department, requesting an appointment for his favorite grandson as a midshipman. Commodore Porter had friends as well as foes in the department; the former supported the petition, while the latter opposed it, and a deadlock was created. The issue was resolved when the matter was called to the attention of President Jackson. The old warrior had been an admirer of the elder Porter for many years, and himself signed the warrant.

So David Dixon Porter, at the age of sixteen, joined the United States Navy. From the outset his attitude was ambivalent. He was determined to recapture the honor he believed his father had lost unfairly, and at the same time he felt superior to most officers. His combat experience was greater than that of many senior lieutenants, and his ego, so similar to his father's, was inflated.

After waiting impatiently until late spring for his orders, Porter was sent to Norfolk, the Navy's fleet headquarters, in early June. There, on his first night in the midshipmen's barracks, he made his presence known by tying tight sailor's knots in the trousers of his peers and filling their boots with water. His fellow midshipmen rewarded him by regarding him as their undisputed leader, a role he accepted as his due.

He was assigned to sea duty on board the old frigate, *Constellation*, commanded by Captain Alexander C. Wadsworth — the flagship of Commodore James Biddle's Mediterranean Squadron. Porter was simultaneously overjoyed and depressed. His father had started his Navy career as a midshipman on the

Constellation, which was a good omen. But Commodore Biddle had been a member of the court-martial board that had suspended his father from active duty, and Captain Wadsworth had been the board's secretary. Therefore, both men were automatically his enemies.

Porter was at least two years older than the other midshipmen, and found his studies so easy that they bored him. The *Constellation*, cruising endlessly through the Mediterranean on a peacetime mission completely lacking in excitement, was a dull place for a youth who craved excitement. And he chafed under the strict disciplines enforced by Captain Wadsworth, whom he despised.

Rebellion was to be expected. When he should have been reading Ovid and Cicero in Latin, he was dashing off his lessons then spending hours in his hammock enjoying the poetry of Lord Byron. To amuse himself and his friends he wrote sly poems, in Byronic style, criticizing the officers. In class he proved that his mind was nimbler than those of the stodgy lieutenants assigned as instructors of the student-officers, and so often confused and humiliated them with his seemingly innocent questions that they soon came to hate him.

He demonstrated boundless ingenuity and imagination, played tricks on the messboys who served the officers' meals, and delighted the enlisted men with letter-perfect imitations of the commodore and the captain. He also revealed his talent as an artist, and his satiric sketches of the officers mysteriously appeared on the bulkheads in the midshipmen's mess. This was too much for his superiors to condone, and a lieutenant named Paulding severely reprimanded him.

Porter, who knew better, blithely replied by telling the officer in detail about the joys of life on board the *Constellation* in his father's time. Paulding confined him to his quarters for the duration of a three-day stay at Valletta, on the island of Malta.

Midshipmen were not allowed to keep alcoholic beverages in their quarters and, although Porter did not drink, he was unable to resist the opportunity to strike back at Paulding. He bought two jugs of cheap, potent brandy-wine from peddlers who came out to the *Constellation* in rowboats, throwing the money down to the men and using a line to haul up the jugs through an open porthole.

Immediately after the frigate sailed from Malta, Porter presented the jugs to Paulding in a mock ceremony attended by the other midshipmen. In angry retaliation, the lieutenant officially cited him for insubordination, which was entered as a permanent black mark against him. A short time thereafter, Porter's warrant as a midshipman came up for its annual renewal, and Captain Wadsworth refused to sign the necessary papers.

The boy was shocked, aware too late that his career in the Navy would terminate unless the warrant was renewed. He appealed to Biddle, but his cause appeared hopeless. The facts in the case were clear, and rarely, if ever, was a captain overruled. Fortunately, the commander of the Mediterranean squadron demonstrated that he bore no personal grudge against Commodore Porter, and after conferring with Captain Wadsworth, he summoned Midshipman Porter to his quarters. The latter was informed that his warrant would be renewed because he was the son of a distinguished Navy hero — and for no other reason.

Porter was confused and abashed. It was difficult for him to feel grateful to men he despised, yet it was equally hard to continue thinking of Biddle and Wadsworth as his father's enemies. Out of the welter of contradictions that raced through his mind one sharp realization emerged: his career was in jeopardy, and it was urgently necessary for him to mend his ways without delay.

During the second year of his tour of duty on board the *Constellation* he proved his mettle. He submitted to the strict disciplines of Captain Wadsworth, became a model student, and obeyed to the letter every foolish and unreasonable order given him by lieutenants who were his intellectual inferiors. He called on his inner reserves of strength, and his conduct became a model of deportment, to the astonishment of the ship's officers.

"Midshipman D. D. Porter," Commodore Biddle wrote in his report to the Navy Department when the *Constellation* returned to New York in December, 1831, "will become an officer worthy of the name he bears."

Porter was overjoyed to find his father at home in Chester. The elder man had returned from Mexico in 1830 at the insistent request of President Jackson, who had appointed him American consul-general in Algiers. Now he was being promoted to a new post, that of chargé d'affaires in Constantinople, a position Jackson had created for a great man he deeply admired. The elder Porter had not yet departed for Turkey, so father and son were reunited.

David Dixon requested and was granted a three months' leave of absence, and returned to the Chester Academy for courses in higher mathematics which were not taught to midshipmen, and which, he believed, were essential to a future navigator. At the end of the period he asked for a second, similar leave, "to devote a little time to the scientific part of my profession." The department granted his request.

Even more important than his studies was his opportunity, as a young adult, to spend time in the company of his father.

They discussed naval matters by the hour, including David Dixon's tactical theory of pressing an attack in battle. And throughout their talks the elder Porter was pleased by signs of his son's growing maturity.

Shortly before the new chargé d'affaires departed for Constantinople, he learned that one of his closest friends in the Navy, Commodore Daniel Tod Patterson, was leaving his post on the Board of Navy Commissioners to take command of the Mediterranean squadron. And Patterson, in a farewell visit to his old comrade, revealed that his flagship would be the newest and largest ship in the Navy, the frigate *United States*.

David Dixon saw an opportunity to serve under a superior who was close to his parents, and brashly requested that he be posted to duty on board the *United States*. According to Navy custom, only senior officers made specific duty requests, and lowly midshipmen went where they were ordered to go. But the Porter name was still influential, and Commodore Patterson quietly let it be known that he approved, with the result that in late May, 1832, Porter received orders to join the *United States*.

He spent the better part of his accumulated wages on a new uniform — a blue coat with gold lace on its collar, a white vest, and tight-fitting buff trousers, shining half-boots, and a handsome dress sword. When he arrived in New York, he also carried with him a full year's supply of bear's oil to dress his hair.

The young man's sudden interest in his appearance was not accidental. He knew that Commodore Patterson would be accompanied by his family, and acted accordingly. The oldest Patterson daughter, Elizabeth — "elderly" at twenty-one — was a friend of his own older sister, and it was the younger girl, George Ann, who excited his interest.

He had known Georgy, who was about a year his junior, most of her life, but not until the Patterson visit to the Porter home in Chester did he suddenly realize that she, too, was growing up. It would not be unfair to Porter to say that Georgy may have been a factor in his request for duty on board the *United States.*

She was graceful and quick, feminine and high-spirited, a girl who loved the sun and did not care if it streaked her brown hair. During the brief visit of the Patterson family in Chester she had shown a great appreciation of David's wit and buoyancy. She had listened intently to his opinions of the Navy's future role in America's growth, and his impetuous nature matched her own. It would be no exaggeration to say that she, too, was looking forward to their reunion.

Carpenters at the Brooklyn Navy Yard were preparing cabins for the use of Mrs. Patterson and her daughters, and a piano had been installed in the family's living quarters on the aft deck. Georgy's luggage arrived in a seemingly endless stream, and Porter, although kept busy by his official duties, could scarcely wait until she came on board with her father, mother, and sister late in June.

Midshipman Porter had bribed a colleague in order to stand watch at the gangway and, dressed in his splendid new uniform, he stood with drawn sword at salute as the commodore was piped aboard. The entire ship's company knew that Georgy's eyes glowed with pleasure when she caught sight of the stern-faced David Dixon standing at rigid attention.

Porter's tour of duty on board the *United States* was one of the more pleasant experiences of his life. He shared a small cabin with two other senior midshipmen, quarters far more luxurious than those assigned to lieutenants on smaller ships.

Even the food was good, and meals served in the midshipmen's mess were remembered by everyone in later years. Commodore Patterson believed that an American flagship sailing in European waters should impress representatives of an older civilization accustomed to pomp, so the ceremonies and rituals were elaborate, as were the entertainments he held for visiting royalty and other dignitaries when in port.

At the same time, the commodore was a disciplinarian, and the spit-and-polish atmosphere was maintained at all times. David no longer found it difficult to conduct himself in a manner befitting an officer and gentleman, partly because the commodore was his father's friend, but also because the other officers on board the flagship were, virtually without exception, admirers of Commodore Porter.

Senior midshipmen attended no classes, but received the equivalent of personal tutoring from the officers in charge of gunnery, navigation, sailing, and ordnance. This gave David the opportunity to gain practical experience, and he was elated when Patterson instituted a new policy that, in effect, gave the senior midshipmen the duties if not the rank of junior officers. Porter stood watch and was allowed to solve day-to-day problems in his own way. He performed so efficiently that the commodore wrote an official letter of commendation that became part of his permanent record in the Navy Department's files.

Patterson was a firm believer in accurate gunnery as the key to victory in battle, and the ships of the Mediterranean Squadron spent a minimum of two to three hours each day in gunnery practice while they were at sea. Porter first worked as a cannoneer, was promoted to the command of a single gun and, eventually, to the status of a battery commander. He was so proficient and worked with such zeal that before his tour of duty ended he acted as chief gunnery officer during a number of exercises.

Nothing he learned from Patterson had greater influence on him than the commodore's devotion to the achievement of accuracy in gunnery fire. The tradition had been inaugurated by John Paul Jones during the American Revolution, kept alive by the Navy's young officers — among them the elder Porter during the undeclared naval war with France in 1812 — and had been stressed during the War of 1812. It was obvious to David Dixon that Lord Nelson had won his great victories because his gunnery had been superior to that of the French and Spanish foes. And it was equally apparent to the young American that his own nation's Navy, smaller than those of the great world powers, would have to rely on rapid, accurate fire in the event the United States became embroiled in a new war with a naval power.

It was inevitable that someone who believed that attack was the cornerstone of victory at sea should accept the theory that gunnery was more important than battle formations and maneuvers. Porter became a perfectionist, and his gun crews were the best in the Mediterranean Squadron. He demonstrated, too, that he had the ability to lead rather than drive men. The seamen who made up his gun crews took pride in their work, and swore by him. Commodore Patterson and his immediate subordinates were convinced that Midshipman David D. Porter would, in due time, become a first-rate officer — a credit to his Navy and his country.

The youth's social life also assumed a new importance, and was centered exclusively around Georgy. When he was not on duty he usually could be found with her in the Patterson salon, or strolling with her on the aft deck. He fell in love with her, making no secret of his emotions, and it was apparent to everyone on board the flagship that she reciprocated his feelings. Commodore and Mrs. Patterson were delighted that their daughter should be forming an attachment to the promising son of old, close friends, and placed no obstacles in the path of their growing relationship.

Porter accompanied the Patterson family, unofficially, on visits to Rome and Jerusalem, and became Georgy's official escort during two weeks of festivities in Naples. The high point came when the squadron put into Constantinople where Chargé d'affaires Porter was the senior representative of the United States. The elder Porter was equally pleased with the romance, and obtained a private audience for his son and prospective daughter-in-law with Sultan Mahmud II, the elderly, autocratic ruler of the Ottoman Empire who saw few foreigners.

As a special favor, the young couple also received a permit to visit the seraglio — the private living quarters of the Sultan's family — and they were fascinated by the harem, which was so far-removed from anything experienced in the United States. Turkish custom did not permit Porter to speak to the sultan's wives, children, or concubines, but the uninhibited Georgy asked countless questions, many of them prompted by her suitor, who muttered to her in an undertone during the tour.

The betrothal of Elizabeth Patterson to Midshipman George M. Bache was announced on board the *United States* at a ball given on August 7, 1833, for Austrian royalty. David and Georgy danced the quadrille and minuet together for the better part of the night, and were inseparable. They held hands at a dawn breakfast served in the senior lieutenants' wardroom, and it was generally believed that their engagement would also be announced in the immediate future.

But their romance was developing too rapidly to suit Commodore and Mrs. Patterson. David and Georgy were too young to marry, they believed, and a senior midshipman's wages were a mere thirty-three dollars a month. Unlike Bache, Porter had no large family fortune behind him.

Rather than discourage the couple, however, the commodore decided it would be wiser to keep David occupied in other ways. The chaplain was directed to establish a school for senior midshipmen; every morning, until noon, they studied mathematics and navigation; every afternoon from one to three they were taught foreign languages by a French schoolmaster. In order to keep Georgy busy, a tutor was hired for her.

Georgy and David were too much in love, however, to be put off. On evenings when the young man was off duty, he climbed over the ship's side along the mizzen chains and entered the aft lounge by the port gallery windows. Georgy met him there, and he courted her to the accompaniment of her father's snores as the commodore enjoyed his after-dinner nap in the adjoining cabin.

Inevitably, the young couple were discovered. The commodore roared, and David gallantly admitted that he and Georgy had been seeing each other secretly. The commodore, impressed by his honesty as well as his refusal to be put off, made the best of the situation. According to a family tradition, he said: "Mr. Porter, when you visit my family, I direct you to come in by the cabin door, like a gentleman."

In February, 1834, Commodore Patterson transferred his red flag to the new ship-of-the-line *Delaware*, and no one was surprised when Midshipman Porter was transferred to the new vessel. He and Georgy had reached a private understanding, with the quiet approval of her parents, but his position was not yet sufficiently secure for them to permit the announcement of their engagement.

In the autumn of 1834, Porter was scheduled to return home to take the examinations that would either win him his commission in the Navy or return him to civilian life. He studied so zealously that Georgy seldom saw him. His future father-in-law guided him, and when the *Delaware* visited Constantinople he also received the benefit of his own father's advice. Their apprehensions were greater than his, and Georgy observed that he would have been far more tranquil had they not studied his textbooks for him, over his shoulder.

Commodore Patterson displayed none of his fears, however, in a letter he wrote to the Navy Department. In it he regretted losing the services of Midshipman D. D. Porter, and predicted that the young man would pass his examinations with ease.

Porter returned home in October, 1834, and after a brief visit with his mother, went to Baltimore. There, in a suite engaged for the purpose by the Navy at the Barnum Hotel, he and nineteen others took exhaustive written and oral examinations that lasted for three days. He passed, but did not distinguish himself — ranking tenth in his class.

On the night he received his commission as a passed midshipman, a rank similar to that of the present-day ensign, he and his classmates adjourned to the bar of the hotel. There, for the first and last time in his life, he drank himself into a state of intoxication. He was now twenty-two years old.

Porter's first assignment as an officer was a true test of his mettle. He was sent to the Brooklyn Navy Yard, which was commanded by his father's lifetime enemy, Commodore James Barron. The commodore assigned him the menial task of clarifying the records of the *Sea Gull*, the little steamer he had first seen as a boy of ten. The work was that of a clerk, and not until many years later did it occur to Porter that perhaps Barron had not been vindictive, but had given him the only work available in a peacetime Navy. Officers of all ranks were resigning and returning to civilian life, and only a Porter would not think of leaving the Navy, no matter how difficult the life.

His work was not only dull, but meaningless. He spent his days in the cramped, dark cabin of the *Sea Gull*, copying the material from her log that he considered essential, but knowing that, no matter how thoroughly he accomplished this task, the ship's days were numbered. She had not gone to sea for years, her engines were badly rusted, and her hull was rotting. "She has become a derelict," he wrote Georgy. "I well remember her in her prime, and want to weep."

He had other reasons, as well, that caused him to feel discouraged. After suffering a bout of what was called "bilious fever," he went home on leave, and discovered that it was becoming increasingly difficult for his mother to keep the Chester house in good condition. Money was scarce, the cost of hired help was rising, and the place was badly in need of repairs. Porter spent several weeks painting the interior, putting in a new floor in his mother's dressing room and rebuilding the hearth in the kitchen out-building. He also took the liberty of writing a frank note to his father in which he said he believed his mother could no longer cope alone with domestic crises.

Commodore Barron had no more work for Porter at the Brooklyn Navy Yard, so he was placed on what was known as a "waiting" status, and remained with his mother, pending receipt of new orders from the Navy Department. Then, in March, 1836, Commodore Patterson returned home to take command of the Washington Navy Yard, and David immediately went to the capital to see Georgy.

The young couple wanted to be married at once, but the Pattersons objected. David earned a minimal base pay of fifty dollars a month, and even if he should be fortunate enough to win a sea duty assignment, he would make only sixty-two dollars. The young man countered with the argument that his older brother, William, had managed to support a wife on that amount. But he was forced to concede that the William Porters had lived in abject poverty.

Georgy, her father said, had never scrimped and had always lived in relative luxury. She would be made to suffer unnecessary hardship on a junior passed midshipman's pittance. The girl herself was willing to ignore her father's warnings, but David could not. The manual labor he had recently performed for his mother was still fresh in his mind, and when he remembered how pale and drawn she had looked, he decided he could not condemn Georgy to a similar fate.

He offered to release her from her pledge to marry him, but she indignantly refused. She was willing to wait for him, she said, until they grew old.

Porter gloomily foresaw just such a possibility. Congress was pinching pennies — not unusual in the last year of a President's term — and was making drastic cuts in Andrew Jackson's budget. Disputes with Indian nations over borders in the expanding West, and the possibility of a war with Mexico over the status of Texas, made it necessary to increase the Army by several regiments, but both the Senate and the House saw the Navy as an expensive luxury. The construction of new ships was halted; training cruises were curtailed; and the department was ordered to cut down target practice in order to save the cost of shot and gunpowder.

Officers of all ranks protested in vain, and it was predicted that many lieutenants and passed midshipmen would resign their commissions rather than wait indefinitely for promotions that might not come. If that should happen, the optimistic Georgy declared, no one was better qualified than her betrothed to step into the vacancies their departure would create.

David was more pragmatic, and had no intention of waiting for his seniors to resign. A chance remark made to him by a classmate sent him to the Navy Department in search of information, and there he learned that a few openings existed in an organization known as the Coast Survey. No senior officer, however, was willing to discuss the subject, and not until David discovered that a classmate, B. F. Sands, and his own future brother-in-law, George Bache, had applied for transfers, did he realize the truth of the situation.

There were vacancies in the Survey for twenty passed midshipmen, and the captains in the Navy Department were remaining silent because they were afraid there would be a stampede. The Survey paid fifty dollars a month in addition to a young officer's base and sea duty pay, and, after three years, was authorized to increase the extra wages to seventy-five dollars. The excited Porter promptly made it his business to learn still more.

Although the Coast Survey used ships and men supplied by the Navy, it was technically a branch of the Treasury Department. As it was being reorganized, no young officer really knew what would be required of him. All applicants, Porter was told, were personally interviewed by F. R. Hassler, Superintendent of the Survey.

Attracted by the prospect of more than doubling his income in three years, he went to Hassler for an interview. The superintendent — a short, myopic man who spoke with a thick German accent — questioned him for several hours about his background, and the meeting turned out to be unique in the young man's experience. Hassler was the only man he had ever met who had never heard the Porter name.

The superintendent said he would study the young officer's record, and abruptly dismissed him. Bache, who had been subjected to similar treatment, tried to encourage him, but Porter spent three agonized weeks waiting for a decision. Finally, late in April, he received official assignment to the Survey, and Commodore Patterson assured him that if he saved his money and earned the higher pay given by the Survey after three years of service, he could marry Georgy.

IV

THE basic mission of the Coast Survey was simple, but its execution was intricate, painstaking, and hazardous. Charts of the waters off the Eastern seaboard of the United States, including the major ports, were notoriously inaccurate and sometimes misleading, which resulted in countless shipwrecks. So many vessels were damaged as they entered the harbors of New York, Boston, and Charleston that merchantmen from Europe frequently preferred to forego American trade. The Survey was therefore ordered to make precise charts of the entire seaboard, and Congressmen from the Eastern states, whose commerce had suffered, were influential in opening the Government's purse strings for the purpose.

The man in sole charge of the operation was F. R. Hassler, an eccentric tyrant with a passion for pinpoint accuracy. A Swiss by birth and education, he had lived in various European nations, among them France and the Kingdom of the Two Sicilies, and had been expelled from both because he not only hated monarchies but had an annoying habit of expressing his views in public. The political climate of the United States was better suited to his convictions.

The personal habits of "the professor," as his subordinates called him, were a never-ending source of astonished amusement to the passed midshipmen on his staff. American wines and cheeses, he said, were "swill," and he always carried with him on his travels a variety of cheeses from Switzerland and Holland, as well as several jugs of French and Rhine wines. Even when dining in taverns and inns, he always produced his own wines and cheeses. He never offered them to companions at meals because, he declared, the American palate was unable to distinguish good from bad.

Always afraid that merchants and innkeepers were cheating him, the professor went to court when he thought his bills were too high. At one time during David Porter's service with the Coast Survey, Hassler was the plaintiff in fourteen lawsuits filed in five different states.

Refusing to admit that he needed eyeglasses for his exacting work of chart-making, Hassler developed his own method of improving his eyesight when he had to examine a chart or map. He used quantities of snuff, and, after sneezing, could see more clearly for a short time. He stored the snuff in every available coat and vest pocket, and the members of his staff took it for granted that any of their work he inspected would be tobacco-smudged.

For all his personal peculiarities, Hassler was a stickler for accuracy, and any member of his staff who failed to meet his high standards was dismissed. Neither Navy officers nor civilians were given a second chance.

The Survey staff was divided into two groups. Navy officers and men spent six months of each year on crowded schooners, and, as the vessels inched their way up and down the seaboard, took endless soundings, measured endless angles between markers set up on shore by civilian surveyors, and drew their preliminary charts. Then, during the winter months, Navy officers and civilian surveyors worked together in two connecting Washington houses that Hassler had leased. There they performed their calculations, collated their geographic data, and drew their precise charts to scale.

The work was tedious and dull, required a knowledge of higher mathematics, and demanded a patience that David Porter had always lacked. He was assigned to the Coast Survey ship *Jersey*, and spent the spring, summer, and early autumn months off the mosquito-ridden swamps of the New Jersey coast. The schooners were small and cramped, and living conditions were barely tolerable. Work done in Washington during the winter was equally boring, unrelieved by excitement of any sort, and even the strongest eyes often blurred and watered as men worked incessantly on their charts.

David did not know it at the time, but he was getting experience that would prove of inestimable value to him at the climax of his career. He was developing an ability to make intricate mathematical calculations quickly, without the need to write them on paper. He became expert in charting channels, and was able to pilot a ship over shallows whose existence he was somehow able to divine. The day would come when these talents would be instrumental in changing history.

There were personal compensations, too. For six months of each year the passed midshipmen on the Coast Survey staff were billeted at the Washington Navy Yard, only a two-minute walk from the commandant's house. David lost no opportunity to spend his evenings with Georgy. And in summer, while cruising along the swamps, he had no chance to spend money, and consequently saved his wages.

Certainly the years Porter spent with the Coast Survey left a permanent mark on his character. Aside from the technical proficiency he gained and the pleasure he felt because of his nearness to Georgy, the experience matured him. His impatience, though curbed, remained close to the surface, always ready to break out. Now, thanks to the painstaking nature of his work, he began to develop a strong quality of self-discipline that, in time, would become second nature to him.

Perhaps the most trying aspect of his Coast Survey assignment was his belief that he was moving no closer to the goals he had set for himself. At best, it was difficult for any officer to establish a reputation in a peacetime Navy, much less erase a blot on his family's name. For someone on loan to a technical agency, the possibility was even more remote. And it was a constant source of annoyance to Porter that a limited number of passed midshipmen were on sea duty with the Navy. He was afraid that, when the need arose, those who had seen the most service on ships-of-the-line, frigates, and schooners would be given the choice assignments. In a letter to his father he expressed the fear that, if war should come again, he would be given dull office work.

His gloomy attitude notwithstanding, he continued to earn a far larger sum than his peers who were enjoying sea duty with the Navy, and at the end of three years' work for the Coast Survey he received the pay increase Hassler had promised him. And he had managed to save almost two thousand dollars, so was at last in a position to marry Georgy.

Through a happy coincidence, Commodore Porter was scheduled to return home for consultations at the State Department. His admirer and sponsor, Andrew Jackson, had persuaded President Martin Van Buren that the American legation in Constantinople was becoming more important than ever before, so the elder Porter was being given the rank of Minister — the highest in the diplomatic service. His wife and children were delighted by his success, and the wedding was set to coincide with his arrival.

David and Georgy were married on March 10, 1839, at St. John's Episcopal Church in Washington, with the groom's parents in attendance, as well as the mother and father of the bride. The Porter family was present in full force, with the exception of David's brother, Theodoric — now a third lieutenant in the Army — who was suffering from a fever and was, therefore, confined to his post in Baton Rouge, Louisiana.

The reception was held at the Navy Yard quarters of Commodore and Mrs. Patterson, and was one of the most important social events of the season. The fathers of the bride and groom captured newspaper headlines the following day.

David and Georgy spent a few weeks together before he returned to duty on the Coast Survey ship, *Washington*, which was making soundings off New Jersey and Long Island. They had expected the separation, but were unprepared for the tragedies that struck both families in the following months.

Commodore Porter returned to Constantinople, leaving his finances in their usual chaotic state, and his long-suffering wife soon discovered that her funds were exhausted. In need of money before she could obtain any from her husband, she was forced to borrow from her elderly uncle. David's correspondence with Georgy in the late spring of 1839 indicates that he was worried about his mother.

Then, that summer, Commodore Patterson unexpectedly dropped dead of a heart attack. David obtained a brief leave of absence to attend the funeral, and then supervised the transfer of his wife and mother-in-law to a small rented house in Washington.

Other tragedies followed. Hambleton Porter, one of David's younger brothers, who was serving as a junior midshipman in the Navy, contracted yellow fever, died and was buried at sea. Henry, another brother, also a junior midshipman, had been drinking to excess, and now was threatened with dismissal from the Navy.

William, David's older brother, scandalized the family when an immigrant servant girl gave birth to a baby he had sired.

The disgrace sent Evalina Porter to bed for several weeks. And the old commodore was so outraged that he sent a formal letter from Constantinople, disinheriting his first-born son. In the eyes of the law, David now became their father's primary legal heir, and the infuriated William wrote him an angry letter claiming that he had influenced the commodore. David denied the false charge, and relations between the brothers became so strained that they were not on speaking terms for years afterward.

In the winter of 1840, while Porter was working at the headquarters of the Coast Survey in Washington, Georgy gave birth to their first child, a daughter, whom they named Georgianne. The infant provided the one bright spot in their otherwise troubled lives. David was suffering from headaches, and it was not discovered until several years later that his eyesight had been impaired by the detail work he had been doing for so long on the Survey's maps and charts. He also developed a liver ailment that plagued him for the rest of his life, and it was probable that, without realizing it, he had contracted malaria while working off the mosquito-infested swamps of New Jersey.

What bothered him more than anything else was the failure of the Navy to promote him. He had expected to be made a lieutenant within weeks after his marriage, but, a year later, the promotion was nowhere in sight. He had accumulated twelve years of seniority in Navy service, and the prospect of remaining a passed midshipman, condemned to Coast Survey work indefinitely in order to support his family, filled him with dread.

His nerves were raw, and one afternoon, in the Coast Survey office, he became embroiled in a meaningless quarrel with a lieutenant, Stephen C. Rowan, also in his late twenties. Angry words led to a scuffle, and the two men had to be separated by their friends. The aroused Porter immediately sent Rowan a formal challenge to a duel, and Rowan promptly accepted.

The Navy's Code of Honor had never been officially disavowed, but no duels had been fought since Commodore Stephen Decatur had been killed by Commodore Barron in 1820. Officers who fought duels could be virtually certain they would be dismissed from the service, even if both parties escaped unscathed. So the seconds, all of whom had been friends for years, persuaded the stubborn Porter and the equally recalcitrant Rowan to exchange a series of letters in which each grudgingly admitted his faults and reluctantly apologized. Porter refused to admit, however, that it would have been foolhardy to jeopardize his career as well as his life. Until the end of his days, David Dixon Porter, like his father before him, considered his honor sacred.

On March 4, 1841, David and Georgy attended the inaugural ball of President William Henry Harrison, and less than forty-eight hours later, the long-awaited promotion materialized. Almost thirty years old, the future four-star admiral finally became a lieutenant. He was so pleased that he made no protest when the Navy Department ruled that officers were required to shave their whiskers from their faces. Although he had previously made a vow that he would not part with his beard, he happily shaved his face clean.

One more year of service with the Coast Survey followed his promotion. He made constant attempts to be returned to duty as a line officer, and in the spring of 1842 he succeeded. He and Georgy were relieved and pleased when he was made second lieutenant and navigation officer of the frigate, *Congress*, which was being sent to join the Mediterranean Squadron.

Late that summer David saw his father for the last time when the *Congress* put into Constantinople. The old commodore was suffering from a severe heart ailment, and knowing that he had little time, gave his son legal control of his affairs in the United States, including a long-pending claim for wages and prize money owed him by the Republic of Mexico. Soon after he and David parted, the old warrior died.

David returned home to face new difficulties. His second daughter, Nina, had just been born, and Georgy was suffering from a mysterious malady that kept her in bed most of the time. The family's physicians were unable to diagnose the ailment.

William Porter was in serious trouble. He had invented a new type of explosive shell that had killed several workmen at the Washington Navy Yard, and, in a fit of temper typical of a Porter, had lashed out so vigorously at his superiors that he had been ordered to stand trial at a court-martial.

David wasted no sympathy on him, writing to their mother, "William must lie in the bed he has made for himself."

His disgust with William was compounded by his brother's lack of compassion for their mother. The commodore's widow was in trouble financially but her firstborn son had filed three separate lawsuits intended to force her to grant him the right to manage her affairs. David had no intention of yielding the responsibility to someone he believed incapable of looking after Evalina's interests.

Her situation was so muddled that he applied to the Navy for a three-months' leave of absence without pay, a rash step that a young officer with an ailing wife and two small children could not really afford to make. Georgy approved, however, and he plunged into the mess with characteristic vigor. His mother owned several small properties in Washington, and he demanded that the people who leased them from her pay their rents or get out. They elected to pay.

He applied, in his mother's name, for a pension from the Navy Department, pointing out that in the War of 1812 his father had destroyed more than a half-million dollars' worth of British shipping, and had almost duplicated the feat when, subsequently, he had driven the pirates from the Caribbean. The Navy regretfully was forced to reject the request on the technical grounds that Commodore Porter had resigned his commission.

Refusing to accept defeat, David sought other sources of income for his mother. Discovering that the post of Collector of Customs for Philadelphia was open, he wrote former President Jackson and other men of influence, and obtained the position for his uncle, Thomas Anderson, who in turn, promised to pay the elder Mrs. Porter five hundred dollars a year out of his salary.

His mother was assured of an income on which she could live, and David was ready to relax, but suddenly found, in the jumble of his father's papers, a note indicating that he had borrowed several thousand dollars from an old and good friend, Commodore John Downes. Downes was a man of means and was not pressing for payment, but David insisted on assuming the obligation, which he considered a debt of honor.

He admitted privately, to his wife and mother, that he had no idea where he would obtain a large sum to pay off the debt. But a lack of funds did not deter him from writing Commodore Downes to assure the old gentleman he thought of the debt as his own, and would repay it in full, with interest.

In spite of his many problems, Porter's professional future began to look somewhat more promising. Agitation was increasing in favor of the admission to the Union of Texas, which had won her independence from Mexico. It was taken almost for granted that if Texas became an American state, war with Mexico would follow. In fact, a number of incidents, including the arrest and detention of several American businessmen in Mexico City, were heating the international atmosphere.

Congress stopped regarding the Navy as an ornamental, useless toy, and influential members of both houses were demanding that new ships be built, that more officers and men be trained to sail them. David played an active role in the Navy's campaign to increase her power, and it is unfortunate that little is known of his specific activities during the early 1840's.

One significant document survives, however — a note he scribbled to his mother. In it he said he had been a member of a special Navy deputation, headed by the secretary, that had called on President Tyler to ask for more ships and men. The President, he said, was sympathetic, and, "I think he is going to give us something to do."

Presumably most members of the deputation were senior officers, and the inclusion of a mere lieutenant in the group was of particular significance. Porter had done nothing to distinguish himself since he had been a Navy officer, so it must be assumed that he was sent to the White House only because his name was David Porter. Undoubtedly this incident was a factor in increasing his desire to become more than his father's son and to establish his own reputation.

But it was difficult to dream of future glory when he was forced to cope with the mundane problems of daily existence. No sooner had he solved his mother's immediate financial needs than his own household was plunged into a minor crisis that required all of his energies. Georgy was ill with a fever, as was his sister-in-law, Elizabeth Bache, whose husband was on duty overseas. Then Mrs. Patterson became ill, and so did the two small Porter children.

The frightened cook and housemaid fled, believing the false rumors that Washington had been stricken by the plague. The concerned and irritated Porter was compelled to apply to the Navy for an extension of his leave of absence. For the next month, as he wrote his mother, he was the "chief cook and bottle-washer" of the household, preparing meals, marketing, and cleaning the house. He had no choice, so he performed his tasks efficiently, but found it difficult to contain his burning desire to return to duty.

The Navy, he knew, had issued secret orders to the Pacific Squadron — in the event of war — to seize the little town of San Francisco, where an important Mexican garrison, the Presidio, was located. The Atlantic Squadron was being prepared for any emergency, and for the first time in years new ships were being constructed. Surely, he reasoned, there would be a suitable combat assignment available for an officer who had earned his seniority through long years of dull, hard labor.

The assignment David received stunned him and almost broke his heart. He was sent to the Navy's Hydrographic Office as an assistant to Lieutenant Matthew F. Maury. The meeting of these two remarkable men was an event of historic significance, and even though Porter was hungry to achieve renown in combat, he instantly recognized the importance of his colleague's work.

Maury, who, several years earlier, had suffered an accident that had made him unfit for sea duty, had developed an interest in ocean meteorology, and was trying to obtain all available data on winds, currents, and other phenomena that affected navigation. In the years ahead he would achieve world fame; he would throw in his lot with the Confederacy during the Civil War, and invent an electric torpedo for harbor defenses that would be adopted by many nations. Eventually, under the terms of a general amnesty, he would return to the United States and, as a professor of meteorology, return to his vital life's work.

The "Mariner's Bible," as the product of his labor came to be called, was culled from ships' logs and other data sent to Washington from the far corners of the earth. Maury's accomplishments in the scant five years he had been in charge of the Hydrographic Office had already won him the unqualified admiration of seamen. Although he was not yet forty years old he had come to be regarded as one of America's most distinguished scientists.

David Porter was fortunate to win an assignment under Maury, and the year he spent in the Hydrographic Office was, in a sense, a postgraduate course that would help make him an exceptionally skilled navigator, at home on the high seas in any weather.

The precise contribution made by David Porter to the achievements of the Hydrographic Office is difficult to determine. The charts of winds and currents that Maury made depended on slow, painstaking efforts, and every fact was corroborated before it was accepted. Certainly Porter had become accustomed to scientific techniques in his years at the Coast Survey, and unquestionably felt at home with Maury. But it is fair to say that, had his reputation depended only on his personal accomplishments in the Hydrographic Office, he would have remained unknown. Maury was the master of his own ship.

Porter couldn't help feeling a sense of discontent even though he recognized the value of the higher education he was acquiring. There were hints, in his sporadic correspondence with his brother, Theodoric, that he was growing tired of schooling and feared he might be forgotten in a Washington office while other men acquired renown at sea.

Meanwhile, the atmosphere in Washington, always sensitive to the country's relations with other nations, was becoming increasingly tense. James K. Polk of Tennessee was elected President on a platform that promised the incorporation of Texas into the Union. President Tyler, not to be deprived of his own place in history, obtained the help of Polk and the dying Andrew Jackson, and in the final days of his Administration, managed to push a bill through Congress annexing the Republic of Texas.

Mexico repeatedly had threatened to go to war under such circumstances, and everyone in a position of authority in the United States expected her to keep her pledge after annexation was completed in July, 1845. The War Department, preparing for any eventuality, sent a corps under General Zachary Taylor to the Mexican border.

Lieutenant Theodoric Porter was a junior officer in that corps, and David scribbled a note to his brother — "I envy the opportunities that await you."

A disciplined Navy officer accepted his situation without complaint, of course, no matter how intense his personal feelings, and Porter said nothing to any of his superiors. He performed his assigned tasks in the Hydro-graphic Office, read the logs of ships' captains fortunate enough to roam the seven seas, and incorporated all data pertinent to tides and currents in his voluminous reports. He continued to suffer the headaches that had plagued him during his last years in the

Coast Survey, and he privately told Georgy that he longed for a respite from the written word.

During this period his private life was less complicated. Georgy had recovered from her mysterious ailment, and was expecting her third child. Porter received an automatic pay increase that made it easier for him to meet his obligations. And his mother needed no financial assistance at the moment, thanks to his continuing supervision of her affairs.

Suddenly, in January, 1846, he was summoned to the office of Captain Arthur A. Bowen, in charge of officer assignments. Was Lieutenant Porter satisfied with his present work?

The question stunned Porter. Officers were rarely asked their opinions, and he didn't know what to make of the unexpected question. But he replied honestly: he respected Lieutenant Maury and recognized the importance of the work being done by the Hydrographic Office, but he wanted action.

Would he be willing to accept a temporary assignment for another Government department? Bowen could tell him only that he would be sent into the field to make a secret investigation of great importance to the United States.

Porter replied that he would accept any assignment given him, but he managed to stress, delicately, that if war came with Mexico, he wanted to go to sea.

Captain Bowen made no promises. But Porter later mentioned in a letter to his mother that the personnel officer had assured him he had been selected by high-ranking officials to perform an unusual and difficult task. If he succeeded, as they believed he would, no reasonable request for duty would be rejected.

All at once the future appeared infinitely brighter, and Porter returned to his work at the Hydrographic Office with a light heart. However, as he once more became immersed in the daily routine of his occupation he began to wonder if the plans of his superiors had changed. January passed, then February, and there was no relief in sight.

V

ON March 8, 1846, Lieutenant David Porter was called to the office of Secretary of State James Buchanan for a secret conference. The amiable and handsome former Pennsylvania Senator, later to become President, told him of a situation in the Caribbean that required an immediate, confidential investigation.

Two years earlier, on the island of Hispaniola, the new Republic of Santo Domingo had been formed, its people having broken away from the Republic of Haiti. Santo Domingo had made an unpublicized request for recognition, financial help, and possible military assistance from the United States. But President Polk wanted to assure himself of the new nation's political and social stability before he committed himself. At the same time, he recognized the value of obtaining an ally in the West Indies when war broke out with Mexico. Accordingly, he wanted a report that would include data on Santo Domingo's economic resources, as well as the suitability of her Bay of Samana for possible use by the United States Navy.

Buchanan offered Porter the opportunity to make the investigation, and the challenge was accepted. The potential of the Bay of Samana for Navy use made it necessary that the mission be conducted by a Navy officer, but there was no indication as to why Porter had been selected. It was true that his work for the Coast Survey had made him an expert on harbors, but nothing in his background had prepared him for a study of economic, political, and social conditions in Santo Domingo. Other officers, most of them older, had served as

Naval attaches at American legations abroad, and it is surprising that the State Department did not turn to one of them.

Porter was not told why he had been chosen, and the files of the State and Navy Departments do not explain the mystery. He asked no questions, however. The assignment was unusual, and would free him from the drudgery of desk work.

On March 15th, one week after his meeting with Buchanan, he left Washington, telling no one his destination. The State Department's desire to maintain secrecy was so great that he traveled to Florida by an indirect route, via Pittsburgh and New Orleans. The commandant of the Navy's Pensacola base assigned him the brig *Porpoise*, under Lieutenant William E. Hunt, who sailed straight to the old city of Santo Domingo, the capital of the little Caribbean republic.

The influence of Spain was still strong in Santo Domingo. Churches, public buildings, and private homes reminded Porter of Mexico City, and Spanish was still the principal language of the inhabitants. Discovering that he had not lost his ability to speak Spanish, he obtained the permission of the government there to conduct his investigation as he saw fit.

After cruising along the coast for two weeks, making charts and sketches of the harbors, he returned to the city to prepare for a difficult trip into the interior. He worked quickly, and before dawn on the morning of May 19th set out across the island, accompanied by a guide and two pack horses. The difficult journey was a test of stamina, and particularly trying to someone unaccustomed to tropical living.

Porter and his guide crossed three rugged mountain ranges and made their way through rain forests of huge mahogany trees. They forded dangerous, rampaging rivers that appeared from nowhere in dry, rock-littered beds after sudden tropical downpours. The plateau of La Vaga, where sweet-smelling grasses grew high and trees bore unfamiliar, delicious fruit, provided a pleasant interlude from hardship. But the tropical valleys proved almost impassable. Snakes, scorpions, and other poisonous creatures were underfoot; the heat of the sun was suffocating; and Porter was constantly forced to cut his own path through a wilderness of bamboo and prickly thickets.

Occasionally he and his companion spent a night in a tiny native village, but more often than not they were forced to string their hammocks in the jungle, chopping away the upper branches of trees so snakes would not drop on them while they slept. When they climbed the narrow mountain passes, the pack horses went first, with Porter close behind them. He carried his revolver, ready at all times to shoot them if they became panicky. It was difficult to obtain fodder for the horses in the mountains, and the animals subsisted on leaves from the stunted trees.

In the gorges, the faint trails crossed the same rivers again and again. Actually, Porter and his companion forded one stream fifty-one times. On occasion he was compelled to swim his horses against strong currents. During one of these ordeals he lost his watch, a sum of American money, and several precious bundles of food. One day he discovered his guide mercilessly abusing the animals, and dismissing the man immediately, proceeded on the journey alone.

Food staples were plentiful, he discovered. The people of the interior lived on breadfruit, bananas, and other vegetation that grew wild. But, aside from an occasional boar, or a bird that was snared by primitive means, meat was unknown. An almost total lack of communication with the coast dwellers prevented the majority of natives from obtaining the fish that were so plentiful in the waters of the Caribbean. By the time Porter reached the village of Puerto Plata on the coast he had developed a sharp appetite for meat.

He was physically weary and run-down when he finally staggered into the village. His left eye was swollen shut from a hornet sting; his face and body were irritated from the bites of other insects; his feet were so badly bruised from wading across river bottoms that every step he took was painful; his legs were puffed to almost twice their normal size. But he had obtained all the information the State Department wanted.

He completely forgot his discomfort when he went aboard the *Porpoise*, which was waiting for him at Puerto Plata. The United States and Mexico were at war! David felt confident that his own experience in the Mexican Navy would assure him an assignment to the Home Squadron, which was stationed in the Gulf of Mexico and would be bearing the brunt of fighting in the war.

On the voyage home he wrote a detailed economic-strategic report which would win him a glowing commendation from Secretary of State Buchanan, but was subsequently ignored by the Administration. He had ample reason to believe that he had succeeded in his mission, and he had proved to his own satisfaction that he could survive in the tropical wilderness.

When he reached Washington he was elated by the discovery that Georgy had given birth to their first son, whom they named David Essex Porter. But his joy was tempered by the news that his brother, Theodoric, had been killed in action. His brother's remains reached Washington a day after he himself arrived, and he went at once to Chester for the funeral. Evalina, the widow and mother of warriors, had grown so accustomed to tragedy that she displayed little emotion.

Immediately after returning to Washington, Porter applied for an assignment with the Home Squadron, mentioning at length his service with the Mexican Navy. But every position in the squadron was already filled, and he was crushed when he was given another scientific post, this time with the Naval Observatory, which studied the stars and used its findings as aids to navigation.

Refusing to let himself be side-tracked, Porter spent the early autumn writing long memoranda to the Secretary of the Navy, suggesting a variety of daring schemes that could destroy Mexico's land-based naval defenses. His ideas were placed on file, and the paperwork at the observatory caused a recurrence of his blinding headaches. Discouraged, he seriously considered resigning his commission, raising funds to buy a sloop, and going off to Mexican waters as a privateer. Only the realization that his obligation to his wife and three children could not permit him to take such financial risks kept him in the Navy.

In November, after spending three months at the observatory, he obtained a respite, and was ordered to take charge of the Navy's recruiting office in New Orleans. Consoling himself with the thought that he would be closer to the scene of actual fighting, he left Washington almost immediately.

By January, 1847, Porter had learned that most volunteers were joining the Army. In spite of his strenuous, unceasing efforts, he had signed only three hundred recruits. The Navy shared his opinion that the operation of the office was a waste of time, and ordered him to proceed by any means available to Vera Cruz, taking his recruits with him. Overjoyed at the prospect of seeing action at last, he chartered a steamer and sailed at once.

Commodore David Conner, commander of the Home Squadron, was a first-rate sailor whose officers and men liked him because he wore colorful, gaudy uniforms. But he was cautious, and, believing his half-trained men incapable of giving a good account of themselves in action, had consistently refused to storm Vera Cruz, which was protected by a powerful fort, San Juan d'Ulloa. Connor was quick to recognize the talents of a good sailor, however, and immediately assigned Porter the post of first lieutenant on board the side-wheel steamer, *Spitfire*, whose captain was Commander Josiah Tattnall, a pugnacious, square-jawed officer.

The captain and his immediate subordinate quickly discovered they held similar views, and Tattnall heartily approved of the schemes Porter proposed — most of them daring plans to sail close to the fort and destroy it with explosives. Commodore Conner refused to take the risks, however, and David again found himself stymied, and confined to a passive role. The war had been in progress almost a year, and although he had reached the coast of Mexico, his activities consisted of drab patrol work.

Then, overnight, the situation changed. Conner was relieved by Commodore M. C. Perry, an imaginative, courageous officer, and the Army sent a corps of ten thousand men to take Vera Cruz. The importance of the operation was emphasized by the fact that command of the corps had been assumed by Major General Winfield Scott, the Army's highest-ranking officer and Chief of Staff.

The sea defenses of Vera Cruz were considered virtually impregnable. In addition to the great fort of San Juan, the city was protected by two smaller fortresses, Conception and Santiago, that stood at either end of the narrow entrance to the harbor. Since the entrance was only eight hundred yards wide, any ships that tried to force their way inside would be subjected to a heavy battering, and the majority of Navy officers believed that their wooden-hulled vessels would be reduced to hulks before they could even come within striking distance of San Juan.

General Scott, the overall commander for the theater of operations, agreed with this estimate. It was essential, however, that he take Vera Cruz. He needed a port as a base for a drive inland; his ultimate goal was Mexico City itself — his first step, the capture of Vera Cruz.

Common sense dictated a landing some miles from the city. If possible, Scott would storm it; if necessary, he would subject it to a siege. The transports carrying the ten thousand men of the Army corps were waiting offshore, and would fresh supplies within a very short time, so plans were quickly perfected, and the landing was made on March 10th.

The *Spitfire* and another steamship, the *Vixen*, plus five sail-driven schooners stood in close to the shore to cover the landing. David, stationed in the bow of the *Spitfire*, had his guns ready for instant action, but not one shot was fired. The Mexicans remained inside the walls of Vera Cruz, and the corps landed unopposed.

A storm that lasted for three days not only delayed the operation but gave the Mexicans time to organize their defenses, and Scott was forced to lay siege to the city. A number of Navy cannon, smaller than his own Army guns, were landed in the days that followed.

Commodore Perry was as anxious as his eager subordinates to win at least a share of glory for the Navy, and on March 22nd he ordered the smaller vessels of his fleet to attack Fortress Santiago at the southern tip of the harbor entrance. The *Spitfire*, which should have been fifth in the line of battle, led the vanguard, and later her captain, supported by his first lieutenant, explained with a straight face that he hadn't read his orders correctly.

Anchoring just beyond the range of San Juan d'Ulloa's powerful cannon, the little steamer fired steadily and accurately at the Mexicans from dawn until a short time before dusk, when she exhausted her ammunition. The return fire from Fortress Santiago was desultory and badly aimed, and at no time was the *Spitfire* in serious danger. The occasion is memorable principally because it was the first time that David Dixon Porter engaged in active combat as an officer in the United States Navy.

He and the other officers of the sub-squadron were not satisfied with their day's work. They had been forced to anchor too far from their target, and Porter volunteered to sound the southern channel into the harbor in order to find better positions for the ships the next day. Taking a crew of eight oarsmen, he went off in Commander Tattnall's gig and managed to penetrate deep into the inner recesses of the harbor without being detected. Had the Mexicans discovered his presence, they could have blown him out of the water, or, cutting off his retreat, captured him.

But he was taking a calculated risk, and his exploit — one of the most daring acts of individual heroism performed in the war — paid handsome dividends.

Returning to the *Spitfire* at two o'clock in the morning, he quickly sketched a working chart of the channel. The officers of the sub-squadron spent the rest of the night holding a secret council of war in Tattnall's cabin. Shortly before dawn they were ready to resume the engagement — in their own fashion. Stripped for action, and riding low in the water because of the heavy loads of ammunition they had taken on board, the

Spitfire and the *Vixen*, each towing two sail-driven schooners, moved toward the harbor.

Instead of halting at the entrance in the positions prescribed by Commodore Perry, however, they sailed inside the harbor entrance, safely using the channel that Porter had charted. The officers and men lining the decks of the other American ships were astonished, and the Mexicans were equally dumbfounded. Commodore Perry, according to a subsequent report made by one of his aides, was rendered speechless.

Withering, concerted fire from the six small American ships made Fortress Santiago untenable, and the Mexicans stationed there abandoned their posts and fled into Vera Cruz. This enabled the *Spitfire* and the other vessels of the sub-squadron to move still closer, and by late morning they reduced the fortress to a shambles. Their mission was accomplished.

But they were still not satisfied. Porter had told his colleagues that Mexican artillery fire was notoriously inaccurate, and they had endorsed his idea of attacking San Juan d'Ulloa. The six ships moved still deeper into the harbor and opened fire on the thick-walled castle. The Mexicans replied at once, and soon shells were dropping into the water around the Americans.

Commodore Perry, who had been watching the action from the quarterdeck of his flagship, ordered the *Spitfire* to withdraw. Even the poorest of enemy gunners could not miss at such close range, and all six ships of the sub-squadron were certain to be destroyed in a prolonged engagement. But Commander Tattnall and Lieutenant Porter were so busy they did not look in the direction of the flagship, and consequently did not see the commodore's signal. By an extraordinary coincidence, neither did the bo's'n or the quartermaster, who ordinarily would have glanced, occasionally, in the direction of the flagship's topgallants. It was equally remarkable that no one on board the other ships of the sub-squadron happened to realize that the commodore was trying to communicate with the *Spitfire*.

The little ships effectively pounded the great fort, ripping a number of holes in her masonry and silencing at least four of her large cannon. Shifting their own positions every time the enemy fire came too close, they miraculously escaped punishment.

The commodore's gig, her small sail raised and sixteen sailors straining at the oars, moved rapidly through the harbor entrance, and, taking a zigzag course to avoid enemy fire, approached the *Spitfire*. A pale-faced passed midshipman, shouting during brief lulls in the roar of cannon, managed to convey the commodore's order to withdraw, so the *Spitfire* no longer had any choice. The sub-squadron retired, with the *Spitfire*, still sending a steady stream of shells at San Juan d'Ulloa, bringing up the rear.

The attack had been so audacious that men on board the other ships of the Home Squadron spontaneously applauded, and so did the officers and men of the merchant vessels anchored in a relatively safe part of the harbor. General Scott, always verbose, sent individual letters of congratulation to the captain and first lieutenant of the *Spitfire*, and every American in the expeditionary force became familiar with the names of Tattnall and Porter. Newspaper correspondents who had witnessed the incident sent glowing accounts home, and readers throughout the United States soon hailed the heroes.

Commodore Perry was in an uncomfortable position. A brave and far-sighted fighting man in his own right, he appreciated the worth of courage and initiative. Until this unexpected incident, the Home Squadron had done nothing to distinguish itself in the war, but now it would share the headlines and the nation's praise with other successful fighting units of the Navy and Army. He had to keep in mind, too, that General Scott, technically his superior, had already congratulated the two officers responsible for the daring assault, and he knew, better than most, that the thin-skinned Scott would be furious if Tattnall and Porter were reprimanded.

On the other hand, the commander and the lieutenant had deliberately disobeyed his specific order to take up their firing position at the entrance to the harbor. When Perry learned that Porter had penetrated the inner reaches of the harbor in a gig to make soundings, there could be no doubt whatever in his mind that the pair had connived behind his back. Officers were expected to obey orders, and the guilty men deserved official reprimands on their permanent records.

Further complicating the issue was the commodore's realization that he would make himself unpopular and slightly ridiculous if he exacted punishment from the officers responsible for the Navy's most gallant act in the campaign. He would also risk stifling the surging spirit of enthusiasm that had swept through the entire Home Squadron.

He solved his dilemma wisely and painlessly by accepting the fiction that no one on board the *Spitfire* had seen his order to withdraw. Thereafter, Perry took no unnecessary risks, and each day personally assigned the steamer her place in the attack force.

Porter, having won a reputation overnight and having tasted glory, would have been unhappy had he been restrained for a prolonged period, but the campaign ended abruptly in less than a week. The Home Squadron maintained her bombardment from the sea until another storm blew up on March 26th.

During the next two days, while the Navy was forced to remain inactive, Army sappers moved their siege lines so close to Vera Cruz that, on the 28th, the commander of the Mexican garrison capitulated.

It was not accidental that the two principal members of the Navy delegation attending the formal surrender ceremonies with the commodore on March 29th were Commander Tattnall and Lieutenant Porter.

General Scott led his corps on a march toward Mexico City, while Commodore Perry assumed responsibility for capturing the principal Mexican towns on the Gulf of Mexico and the main rivers feeding into it. On April 18th, with the commodore himself on board the *Spitfire* as it sailed up the Tuspan River, Porter gave a convincing demonstration of his superb gunnery by knocking out the Mexican artillery batteries on the cliffs protecting the garrison town of Tuspan. The Mexicans fled from the town, and American Marines occupied it.

In June the Home Squadron faced a more difficult task. The port town of Frontera, at the mouth of the Tabasco River, was already in American hands, but was plagued by frequent guerrilla attacks, so Commodore Perry decided to clear the entire seventy-mile length of the river and, in particular, capture the city of Tabasco, which was still a Mexican stronghold.

Sixteen miles below the city the small vessels of his assault force were halted by obstructions the Mexicans had placed in the river, and the commodore proceeded by land toward his goal with a force of one thousand Marines and sailors. Porter, however, refused to be deprived of a share in the glory, and performed his second spectacular exploit of the war.

Engineers placed sealed drums of gunpowder at the base of the underwater piles of logs, then detonated the charge, sending a geyser of mud and water high into the air and breaking the logjam. Porter stationed himself in the bow of the *Spitfire*, summoning every available hand to help him and, using makeshift tools, cleared a path for his ship and the *Vixen*.

The two steamers resumed their voyage upstream at full speed. When they reached Tabasco, Porter went ashore with a force of eighty-six sailors and two passed midshipmen. Daringly scaling the walls of the city's protecting fort, they forced the surrender of the startled garrison. Not one man was killed or injured in the swift assault.

Two hours later, when Commodore Perry and his weary attack force arrived after a long march through steaming jungles, they saw the American flag flying from the ramparts, and were greeted by Porter and his mud-spattered seamen.

Again Lieutenant David Porter won his share of headlines in American newspapers, and people throughout the United States realized he was a fighting son of a fighting father. He also won more concrete rewards. Commodore Perry gave him a warm commendation that became part of his permanent record, and he was made captain of the *Spitfire*. For the first time in his thirty-four years he was the commander of an American warship.

The months that followed were anticlimactic. Aside from dispersing a few guerrilla bands with gunfire, Porter's principal occupation was that of supervising commercial traffic in Mexican ports the Americans had captured. Neither he nor his ship saw any more real action, and when General Scott took Mexico City, the war came to an end. The United States acquired vast new territories extending to the Pacific, and the exploits of other heroes overshadowed those of the *Spitfire's* commander.

By the end of the year Porter was detached from his command and ordered home. In a final letter to Georgy, which actually arrived in Washington a few days after he himself reached his destination, he said, "Had I been stationed elsewhere I would have fared better. It is true that I won a small measure of attention, but my achievements contributed little to the winning of the war, and soon will be forgotten, I fear."

His gloom deepened on his homeward journey. Other officers, whom he met in New Orleans and who made at least part of the trip with him, shared his conviction that the Navy would revert to its peacetime economies. Only a few berths at sea would be available, and officers who had commanded their own ships would find it difficult to take subordinate positions. Most of them, in all probability, faced arbitrary retirement.

By the time Porter reached Washington he was convinced that his career in the Navy was in danger of being terminated. Newspapers he had read in Pittsburgh indicated that the Navy was planning to sell its steamships in the immediate future because sailing vessels were less expensive to operate. The policy was short-sighted, he believed, but there was nothing he could do to change the situation. In fact, he would be fortunate if his superiors allowed him to remain on active duty.

In a letter to his mother, intended for her alone, he confided that he would not remain in the Navy if he were given another dull office assignment: "I am first and foremost a sailor, and in one way or another, even if it be as a civilian, I shall spend the rest of my life at sea, in command of my own ship. Having known command, I cannot be satisfied with less, and will not accept less."

His anger and fear were temporarily forgotten when he was reunited with his family and caught up in the whirl of domestic activities: Georgy had been ill, but was now well again; both of the girls had caught the mumps. But his son, whom everyone called Essex, was in robust health, and his father was delighted with him.

"In spite of my own disappointments," Porter wrote his mother, "and no matter how precarious my own vocational future may be, I can contemplate no future for Essex other than that of an officer in the Navy."

VI

ON January 10, 1848, Lieutenant David Porter was reassigned to the Coast Survey, and that night wrote a letter resigning from the Navy. He did not submit the letter, however, because, early the next day, he learned of circumstances that caused him to change his mind. One was his assignment as captain of the schooner *Petrel*; it was difficult for him to resist a sea command of his own.

His other reason for remaining in service was the nature of his mission, which challenged him. He was directed to survey the Hell Gate and Buttermilk Channels in New York Harbor and immediately recognized the importance of the task. Hundreds of ships passed through Hell Gate every week, making it the busiest harbor channel in the United States. It was also one of the most hazardous. Each month dozens of ships were damaged by underwater shelves of rocks. In addition, there had been a number of sinkings. Hell Gate was the graveyard of international shipping and was threatening the future of America's largest city and foremost port.

The man who accurately charted the harbor and eliminated the hazards to shipping would acquire a permanent place in history — and David Porter realized this. Buttermilk Channel, between Governors Island and Brooklyn, was considered unsafe by both the Navy and commercial shippers, so neither used it. Porter decided that the establishment of a practical route by ocean-going ships, including large Navy vessels, would make a favorable impression on his superiors.

A personal problem also tempered his decision. As Georgy was carrying her fourth child, the father of a still growing family needed more money. The prospect of doubling his income unquestionably influenced his decision to rejoin the Coast Survey for a limited time.

He spent part of the winter sailing alone, repeatedly, through both Hell Gate and Buttermilk Channel in order to familiarize himself with details of contour that would make his later task easier. Such investigations would have been dangerous at any time of year, and a man venturing out alone in a small sailboat was taking extraordinary risks, but Porter showed his usual lack of concern for his own safety. When there was a task to be done, he gave it priority, and let no other considerations interfere.

When the warm weather came, he put out in the *Petrel* with a crew of experts, and spent six weeks surveying Hell Gate; the importance of his mission was underlined by accidents involving fifty-three ships during this period. The New York Chamber of Commerce was so anxious to begin blasting the channel that he made progress reports to the Treasury Department as he worked his way through the channel, taking soundings. Newspapers in New York and other major cities printed daily articles on his findings.

To the astonishment of everyone concerned, Porter's survey of Buttermilk Channel was completed in ten days. He had discovered a passage that was usable, he declared, and neither blasting nor dredging would be necessary. The New York newspapers hailed him as a genius, but he had made the job look so easy that Secretary of the Treasury, R. J. Walker, was skeptical. He challenged Porter to make a trial trip with him through both channels on board an ocean-going vessel. The offer was accepted.

On September 22nd, Secretary Walker and David Porter went aboard the Treasury's revenue steamer *Jefferson*, accompanied by a delegation of ship owners, representatives of the New York Chamber of Commerce, a number of scoffing harbor pilots, and a large group of newspaper correspondents. Porter's reputation was at stake, but he was completely unconcerned.

The *Jefferson* was an unwieldy ship and, because she responded awkwardly to her helm, needed more room than most ships for turns. She was, therefore, considered ideal for the purpose of the test. She made her passage through Hell Gate and back without incident, her captain and a harbor pilot following the line indicated in Porter's charts with a sense of growing excitement pervading the company.

A stiff northwest wind was blowing and the tide was unfavorable by the time the *Jefferson* started her run through Buttermilk Channel. The experiment was further complicated by the presence of a lumber ship, with planks protruding from her sides, lying at anchor in the middle of the passage. But the experiment was carried out smoothly, and Secretary Walker extended his formal congratulations to Lieutenant Porter. New York's newspapers, much less reserved in their reaction, hailed him as a hero.

Almost simultaneously, Porter received word that Georgy had given birth to their second son, Carlisle Patterson. Naturally he was anxious to return to Washington, but an unexpected business offer detained him in New York. The discovery of gold in California had created a tremendous demand for transportation to the Pacific and, although every available windjammer and other type of sailing vessel had been pressed into service by the shipping companies, the clamor was still unresolved.

It was obvious that steamships, which traveled more rapidly and held far more passengers than sailing ships, were needed.

Only a few large steamers had been built, however, and there was a lack of experienced sailors to man them. John J. Aspinwall, head of the private banking firm of Howland and Aspinwall, had inaugurated a shipbuilding program and was busy recruiting crews for the ships he already owned.

The largest of these was a steamer of ten thousand tons, the *Panama*, which had been making test runs out of New York, and soon would be ready for her maiden voyage to San Francisco by way of Cape Horn. Aspinwall made it his business to be present at the runs of the *Jefferson* through Hell Gate and Buttermilk Channel, and of course was aware that Porter had commanded a steamer during the Mexican War.

Therefore, the seasoned Navy officer was the logical candidate for the post of master of the *Panama*, and Porter was surprised when the banker offered it to him. The opportunity was greater than he had ever imagined, and the experience at sea to be gained would give his Navy career a great boost.

Returning to Washington, he applied to Secretary of the Navy John Y. Mason for a leave of absence, explaining that he would be far more useful as an officer in the Navy after sailing the *Panama*, Mason, who was hoping to order more steam-propelled vessels for the Navy in spite of the opposition posed by economy-minded members of Congress, granted the leave.

Porter spent several weeks putting his mother's financial affairs in order once again, repairing her property, and obtaining rental money owed to her. Then, after attending the christening of his son, Carlisle, he hurried back to New York, donned a civilian sea-going officer's uniform for the first time, and interviewed members of his crew.

He inspected his ship, found her seaworthy and, on February 15, 1849, put out to sea. Among his cabin passengers was a distant cousin of Georgy's, Henry Livingston, one of New

York's most prominent financiers. Two others were young officers with whom he became friendly — Joe Hooker and William H. Emory, both of whom would become major generals in the Union Army during the Civil War. All available space in the steerage was occupied by men of every class and station anxious to join in the hunt for gold.

Four days after leaving New York, Porter was forced to turn back when one of his engines became partly disabled. His passengers were bitterly disappointed. However, they did not know the determination of their captain, who quickly supervised the making of repairs, and then took on an additional cargo of tools and spare parts so he would be prepared if another breakdown occurred at sea.

The *Panama* made a nonstop southward voyage through the Atlantic, safely navigated the Straits of Magellan during the worst season of the year, and headed northward again in the Pacific. Porter overtook scores of sail-driven ships on the voyage, and each time his passengers celebrated. When he reached the little town of San Francisco on June 4th, the passengers presented him with a gift, and hundreds of people lined the shore to watch him berth the ship.

He turned over the *Panama* to officials of the new Pacific Mail Steamship Company, and returned on board as a passenger as far as the Isthmus of Panama where people who had crossed from the Atlantic side got on board. Porter debarked at this point and made his way through the jungles of Panama in the blazing heat of midsummer — his experience in Santo Domingo standing him in good stead — and eventually obtained a berth on a mail steamer bound for New York.

A representative of the shipping company of Law & Roberts met him at the dock in New York and offered him the captaincy of a new steamer, the *Georgia*, not yet commissioned, which would make the run from New York to Panama by way of Havana. Porter was not only eager to accept, but wanted to take charge immediately so he could utilize what he had learned about steamers on the *Panama* and personally supervise the installation of the ship's double engines.

He hurried to Washington, and was surprised to receive a cool reception from President Zachary Taylor's Secretary of the Navy, William B. Preston. There were technicalities to be observed, the prim secretary told him: the *Georgia* would carry United States mail, and therefore would be subsidized in part by the Government, which could not accept her until she was operational. Therefore, no Navy officer could be assigned to her until she had made her sea trials and won official Government approval.

Porter urged the waiving of all technicalities. No officer of his rank ordinarily was given such opportunities, and he was desperately anxious to obtain the post. Preston was adamant, however, and told him to apply again, if he wished, after the *Georgia* was approved by Government inspectors. Porter went home, bitterly angry, and promptly succumbed to the fever he had contracted during his journey on foot through the jungles of Panama.

His convalescence was protracted, and by the time he was completely recovered, in January, 1850, the *Georgia* had been completed and approved by the Government. Again he submitted his request for a leave, in order to command her. This time Preston agreed, perhaps because he could find no valid reason to object.

Accordingly, on January 26, 1850, Captain David D. Porter, temporary civilian, took command of the *Georgia*. On the surface he observed the amenities, inviting passengers to join him at his table for meals and allowing those whom the ship's owners believed important to inspect his engine rooms. He soon proved, however, that he was no ordinary civilian master, and constantly tried to improve his own speed records.

The *Georgia* stopped at Charleston and Savannah for mail and passengers. Discovering that he lost a great deal of valuable time by sailing into port, he wrote to the owners, suggesting that transfers be made at sea, by tender. Law & Roberts displayed no interest in setting speed records, however, and when his requests were ignored he decided to take the initiative and settle the issue as he saw fit.

Thereafter, passengers disembarking at the two Southern ports on the voyage to Havana were put into small boats along with the mail — no matter how they felt about it — and on northbound trips were picked up in the same way. Some — including those who became seasick in small craft or disliked being doused by salt spray — sent indignant protests to the owners, who relayed them to the master of the *Georgia*. Porter, by this time increasingly convinced that the greatest value of steamships lay in the speed they could achieve, continued to halt briefly in the open sea, and blithely ignored the complaints.

He proved to be a distinctive captain in other ways, too. Merchant marine crews in the mid-nineteenth century were indifferent, informal, and often sloppy. Their attitude outraged a Navy officer who believed that instant obedience was the first commandment on board ship, and that any officer or sailor who disregarded it should be discharged at once. The *Georgia* soon became the most efficient merchant vessel in the Atlantic, and the discipline enforced by her captain fully lived up to Navy standards.

The chief engineer of the *Georgia* was directed to keep a precise log, and when an inspection of his records indicated that he had been lazy, David threw him into the brig. Three assistant engineers who were sympathetic to their superior refused to keep the log in the manner prescribed by the captain, so Porter placed them in irons, too. All four were dismissed, without pay, the moment the *Georgia* returned to New York.

The crew grumbled, of course, and the steamer's owners were inclined to agree that the captain was a martinet. But the *Georgia*'s sailing record surpassed that of any other steamer, and her bills for fuel and repairs were lower. After due consideration, the directors of Law & Roberts ordered the other ships in the line to observe Captain Porter's strict measures of discipline.

Other companies, noting that Law & Roberts made higher profits, encountered fewer labor problems, and maintained a higher degree of efficiency, soon followed suit. Had David Porter accomplished little else, he was responsible for the installation of genuine discipline in an American merchant service that had become slipshod and careless. The sharp improvement of the civilian accident record at sea was also a direct result of his unyielding efforts.

Throughout his civilian service he continued to think of himself as a lieutenant in the Navy, and at the end of each voyage submitted a full report to the Secretary of the Navy, stressing the manner in which his ship had performed. These reports proved of great value in training officers when the Navy shifted from sail-driven vessels to steam.

In fact, the *Georgia* herself became a Navy training ship. Unable to obtain civilian officers of the caliber he demanded, Porter asked the Navy Department to grant leaves, similar to his own, to junior officers for the purpose of serving under him. The Navy, aware of the benefits involved, readily complied.

Perhaps it was inevitable that the Porter sense of patriotism and honor should create an international incident. In the autumn of 1852, while temporarily in command of a steamer called the *Crescent City* while the *Georgia* was undergoing repairs, he brought the United States to the brink of war with Spain. A Havana newspaper reported that the purser of an American merchant steamer — a man named Smith — was maliciously charging Spanish colonial authorities with the illegal jailing of more than a thousand Cuban patriots.

When the *Crescent City* put into Havana, Spanish officials came on board to determine whether her purser was responsible for casting false aspersions on the processes of Spanish justice. Porter questioned Smith, who denied that he was guilty, and the captain relayed this information to the officers.

A few weeks later, when the *Crescent City* next reached Havana, a group of Spanish Army officers came on board with a demand from the Spanish governor-general. Smith, they said, was required to deny the charges, in person and in writing. Porter not only refused to let his purser testify, but ordered the Spaniards off his ship.

The offense, he declared, was merely alleged, and had not been proved. Furthermore, he said, even if Smith had been responsible, the comment had been made on American soil, and the Spanish authorities in Cuba had no jurisdiction in the case. The irate governor-general ordered a Spanish gunboat to cruise beside the *Crescent City* until she left Cuban waters. Porter, refusing to be intimidated, retaliated by mounting cannon fore and aft while he sailed into international waters.

The *Crescent City*'s destination was New Orleans, and a few hours after he docked there the city erupted in a series of parades and mass meetings. Porter, keeping his plans to himself, quietly took on passengers, supplies and mail, and returned to Havana.

He reached the city before dawn on October 14th, and, rather than call attention to himself by taking on a Spanish pilot, personally guided his ship to her berth. Subsequently he learned the accuracy of what he had guessed: a Spanish warship had been lying in wait to intercept him, but he had slipped past her in the dark.

The governor-general posted a guard on the dock, forbade the discharge of passengers and mail, and refused Porter's request for an interview with the United States consul. Calmly, as though this were an ordinary halt on an ordinary voyage, Porter ordered his crew to paint the *Crescent City*'s hull.

Several hours later, an official of the steamship line and an American assistant consul were allowed to visit the ship, and Porter gave them a blistering written message to the governor-general in which he repeated his previous stand, but in still stronger terms. Then, sailing out of the harbor in defiance of two gunboats that had been directed to hold him in port, he deliberately fired a salute to the American flag flying from a staff on the consulate lawn.

When the *Crescent City* reached New York, thousands of people were on hand to cheer her captain, and a delegation of citizens tried to present Porter with a handsome dress sword. He refused, saying he did not believe Navy officers should accept gifts for doing their duty.

The United States Government was alarmed. Porter was called to Washington to report the incident in detail; two warships were sent to Havana to investigate and prevent a repetition of the affair; and Smith, the purser, complied with a State Department request to deny — in writing — that he had made derogatory remarks about Spain.

Neither Washington nor Madrid wanted war, and a flurry of diplomatic exchanges buried the incident in a sea of words. Porter returned to the command of the *Georgia*, and the affair was forgotten.

In the late spring of 1853, Porter suffered a recurrence of malaria, and was forced to take a leave of absence while he again recuperated from the debilitating ailment. During his convalescence he decided he had nothing more to learn as commander of the *Georgia*, and contemplated requesting a return to Navy duty. Then Georgy gave birth to her fifth child, Elizabeth, so her husband hesitated: a Navy lieutenant's pay was inadequate to support a large family.

Out of nowhere, early in 1854, he received a letter from the Australian Steamship Company, offering him the captaincy of a new steamer, the *Golden Age*, now berthed in New York, which newspapers in the United States and England had been ridiculing. Her prow was blunt; her cabin decks sat high above the water line; and, in a final touch of absurdity, she operated by means of paddle wheels, like a Mississippi River steamer.

Porter inspected the ship and, convinced that she could set new speed records, applied to the Navy for the right to accept. His request was granted, and he promptly set a new record for an Atlantic crossing.

But this was just the beginning. He made the voyage from Liverpool to Australia, rounding the southern tip of Africa and cutting through the Indian Ocean, in an astonishing fifty-six days, beating the previous record by a full thirty days. Newspapers throughout the world hailed the achievement, and the American community in Melbourne gave him a magnificent banquet. Thus, at the age of forty-one he finally achieved the international renown he had been seeking since his youth.

A celebrity, followed by crowds wherever he went, he remained in Australia for several months, carrying passengers and mail from Melbourne to Sydney, and back. Other steamers made the run in four days, so it amused him to cut the time in half, and his fame increased. The owners of the *Golden Age* paid him handsome bonuses and begged him to accept permanent employment with them, but he was anxious to rejoin his family because Georgianne, his eldest daughter, had become seriously ill. He returned home by the shortest route, sailing to Tahiti, from there to Panama, then taking a mail steamer from the Atlantic side.

Using a portion of his profits, Porter bought a house on East 33rd Street in New York City, hoping that the climate would be more beneficial to Georgianne than the ever-humid Washington, but she died a short time after the family moved in. The grief of Porter and Georgy was only partly relieved by the birth of another son, Richard Bache.

In the late summer of 1854, the Navy Department returned the renowned Lieutenant David D. Porter to active duty, his superiors having belatedly recognized that he was an extraordinary officer. His record showed that he had displayed courage at Vera Cruz, and the *Crescent City* incident had demonstrated his stubborn sense of honor. The commodores were impressed by his ability to instill discipline in civilian crews; his speed records spoke for themselves, and so did the vast sailing experience he had acquired. Equally important, the Navy valued his zeal, energy, sense of responsibility, and eagerness to undertake ventures that were out of the ordinary.

It was taken for granted that he would be promoted to higher rank whenever an appropriate opening occurred.

Anticlimactically, however, Navy physicians ordered him to take a prolonged sick leave to recover from his last bout of malaria, his condition having been aggravated by his arduous voyages on the *Golden Age*. Early in 1855 he returned to duty, and his first assignment, in April, was a strange one.

Camels had been used as cavalry mounts in the Crimean War, and Congress had appropriated funds for the Army to acquire a number of them, to be used in Texas on an experimental basis. During the next two years Porter made two long voyages to the eastern Mediterranean, in command of the storeship *Supply*, to purchase camels and bring them back to the United States.

He was successful in carrying out the bizarre assignment, which paid him handsome personal dividends. While berthed in Constantinople he accepted the invitation of the British to make an observation trip to the Crimea, and there was deeply impressed by a French floating battery sheathed with armor plating. He constructed a model of it, and also made miniatures of new underwater explosives being utilized by both the British and French. After conducting a number of simple tests with the equipment at hand, he sent the models and voluminous notes to the Navy Department, where the material aroused considerable interest.

In 1857, after returning home, he finally succeeded in his campaign of many years to win a government pension for his mother. A short time later, in the spring, he was assigned to a post at the Portsmouth, New Hampshire, Navy Yard, and remained there for more than two years.

The best that could be said of this period was that the New Hampshire climate was good for his health. His second daughter, Nina, died there, and Georgy suffered from occasional melancholy, although she had two more children, Theodoric and Elena. Porter's duties were light, his boredom pervasive, and he became thoroughly dissatisfied with his lot.

He had good reason to be unhappy. He was forty-six years old, and for eighteen years had held the rank of lieutenant. His promotion to commander was long overdue, but nowhere in sight. An inspection tour, made as a member of a special board, that took him to every navy yard on the Atlantic seaboard, did nothing to relieve his dissatisfaction.

Only a very few small ships were being built. Repair facilities were inadequate and old-fashioned. The little Washington Yard was the only one that could repair and recondition steam engines. A new Congressional economy campaign forbade repair work of any kind costing more than a thousand dollars, so warships of every classification, from ships-of-the-line to small bomb ketches and messenger sloops, either rode at anchor, rotting, or were being decommissioned.

No two yards used the same operational systems. This naturally resulted in confusion, duplications of effort, and unnecessary expense. Morale was low, and officers, enlisted men, and civilian employees took no real pride in their work. Many sailors were men of the lowest order, including thieves and gamblers who had enlisted in order to escape trial in the civilian courts of the states. Worst of all, the older, senior officers had no desire to change the status quo, and actively discouraged technical innovations and the application of new inventions.

John Ericsson, who would be hailed within a few years as the "father" of the ironclads, was either ignored or treated as a wild dreamer. Only a minor miracle made it possible for Lieutenant John Dahlgren, of the Navy Bureau of Ordnance, to develop and produce a new muzzle-loading cannon that would prove to be the most effective gun in Naval history. And Lieutenant Maury was able to publish his Mariner's Bible only because many of the higher-ranking officers were unaware of the existence of an officer whose bid for fame they would have resented because of his junior rank.

David Porter could see no future for himself in the Navy, although he continued to love the service. At this critical low point in his life, late in 1859, the Pacific Mail Steamship Company approached him with an attractive offer — a permanent, well-paid post as captain of the largest and most modern of American passenger steamships, which would soon be built. Her keel had not yet been laid, and her construction would not be completed for another twelve to eighteen months, so there was no need for him to make an immediate decision.

He was tempted, of course, and his desire to accept was strengthened in 1860, when he was transferred back to Washington, where he discovered that the most influential senior officers were still thinking in terms of sail-driven ships rather than the modern fleet of steamers that he considered essential for the operation of an efficient Navy.

The election of Abraham Lincoln as President of the United States in the autumn of 1860 made it even more difficult for Porter to retain much faith in the future of the Navy. Prominent Southerners were making no secret of their plans to secede from the Union, and one of the most outspoken was Senator Jefferson Davis of Mississippi, who had become Porter's close friend. In fact, at a dinner party held at the Senator's house, Mrs. Davis half-jokingly offered Porter an admiral's rank if he would cast his lot with the South.

Other Navy officers were already taking active steps to align themselves with what would soon become the Confederacy. Commander Tattnall, who had been Porter's commanding officer at Vera Cruz, resigned his commission and moved South. Commander William Porter, David's mercurial older brother, bought a house in Richmond for his family.

Troubled and bewildered, Porter decided to straddle the issue. He would accept the civilian offer, and in the meantime take a position with the Coast Survey in California.

VII

ON December 20, 1860, South Carolina seceded from the Union, and one by one the other Southern states followed her lead. By the time President Lincoln was inaugurated on March 4, 1861, a civil war appeared inevitable. Troops loyal to the Union still maintained a precarious hold on forts at Charleston, Pensacola, and Norfolk, but their fall appeared imminent. The greatest danger threatened Fort Pickens, at Pensacola, where the Navy Yard had already been occupied by Confederate forces.

Porter, deeply disturbed but still determined to leave for his Coast Survey post in the Pacific within the next few weeks, discussed the Pensacola situation from a purely technical standpoint with his next-door neighbor, Army Captain Montgomery C. Meigs. Both believed that the dispatch of a secret expedition could relieve Fort Pickens and recapture the Pensacola Navy Yard.

Meigs mentioned the matter to several superiors, and on April 1, only a few days before Porter was scheduled to depart for the Pacific, he and Meigs were summoned to a private conference with Secretary of State William H. Seward. At the latter's request they repeated their conversation, and Seward was sufficiently impressed to take them, then and there, to the White House.

President Lincoln listened carefully and, although his knowledge of military and naval affairs was slight, he recognized the sincerity and competence of both officers. Approving their plan, he allowed them to write orders for his signature while they were still in his office, Porter having argued that the plan could succeed only if it was kept a closely guarded secret and that secessionist sympathizers would learn of it if the orders were processed through the usual Navy and War Department channels.

Porter was given command of an old side-wheel Navy steamer, the *Powhatan*, then in New York awaiting decommissioning, and was authorized to take on as many cannon and as much additional ammunition as he deemed necessary. Meigs was made the head of an assault force, and the entire operation was placed under the command of an elderly, conservative Army officer, Colonel Harvey Brown, whom both younger men intended to ignore.

When David left for New York, accompanied by his eldest son, Essex, who would serve with him as captain's clerk, Georgy told their friends he was leaving for his post with the Coast Survey in California. Arrangements were made in New York for sailing within the week, and were kept so secret that only two or three officers knew the secret. In any event, Porter's personal doubts were resolved: he would remain loyal to the Union, where his basic sympathies had lain since the start of the controversy.

Shortly before sailing he received a telegram from Seward, who was calling off the expedition, in large part because the realization that Secretary of the Navy Gideon Welles knew nothing of the plan made him nervous.

Porter, however, had no intention of halting at the last moment, and, a few minutes before sailing, sent the Secretary of State a blunt reply: "*I received my orders from the President and shall proceed and execute them.*"

For Pickens, at the western end of a forty-mile-long sandspit called Santa Rosa Island, dominated the entrance to Pensacola Harbor, and on the mainland, opposite it, were two somewhat stronger forts, McRee and Barrancas, while a few miles to the east stood the Pensacola Navy Yard. On his voyage southward, which was slowed by gales, Porter studied the charts and maps of the area, heartened by the knowledge that a small Union force still held Fort Pickens, and that Union reinforcements awaited him on board several smaller vessels — the largest of them, the *Brooklyn*.

His basic plan was simple: he hoped to gain admission to the harbor entrance disguised as a civilian mail ship, while Colonel Brown and Captain Meigs discharged their troops at Pickens from the chartered steamer, the *Atlantic*, on which they were sailing south.

The voyage of the *Powhatan* lasted eleven days, and Porter ordered his gun crews to practice by the hour, relieving them only when they saw Confederate shipping. His disguise was so effective that he was not challenged, although Fort Sumter was shelled, forced to surrender, and evacuated during this period.

When the *Powhatan* and the *Atlantic* reached their destination, the six hundred troops on board the chartered steamer began to debark at Fort Pickens, and cannon were unloaded from both vessels to bolster her defenses. Porter was anxious to sail into the harbor at once, to challenge the Confederate troops on the mainland, but the cautious Brown ordered him to wait.

The Confederates, however, had no intention of permitting the Union Army and Navy to strengthen Pickens, and sent a small flotilla of launches and schooners from Fort Barrancas to disrupt the landings on the island. Porter fired a single shell from one of the *Powhatan*'s eleven-inch guns, and when it exploded directly over the boats, showering metal fragments on them, the Confederates took the hint and turned back.

Porter promptly established a blockade of the harbor entrance, in order to prevent the enemy at McRee and

Barrancas from obtaining supplies and reinforcements by sea. This move was opposed by Captain H. A. Adams, an elderly naval officer who had been in charge of the besieged Fort Pickens's defenses for three weary months. Although Adams was the senior officer, the impatient Porter accepted full responsibility for the blockade. The question was solved on May 12th with the receipt of a copy of President Lincoln's order establishing a formal blockade of all Southern-held ports.

Two weeks later, Captain William McKean, an energetic officer, arrived on board the steamer *Niagara* to relieve Adams. As eager as Porter was to see action, he ordered the *Powhatan* and *Brooklyn* to blockade the Pensacola forts while he himself, on the *Niagara*, sailed off to blockade the city of Mobile.

The *Powhatan* drew first blood when Porter intercepted a commercial schooner from New Orleans, the *Mary Clinton*, and sent her off to New York with a prize crew aboard. Under the ancient laws of the sea still in force, he, his officers and men would share in the proceeds of her sale.

A message from Captain McKean promised the *Powhatan* and the *Brooklyn* considerably more activity than they had yet seen. Fort Pickens had been made strong enough to defend herself, McKean decided, and ordered Porter to take the two ships to the mouth of the Mississippi and establish a blockade of New Orleans.

No officer — not even a David Dixon Porter on the verge of winning everlasting fame — could meet that challenge with the equipment at hand. Four powerful warships, each of them commanded by exceptionally competent former commanders in the United States Navy, were being outfitted at New Orleans by the Confederates and soon would go to sea. Any one of them was strong enough to match the challenge jointly posed by the *Powhatan* and the *Brooklyn*.

Even without the threat of these new ships, Porter could not have accomplished his mission. The waters of the Mississippi spread out into four separate channels below New Orleans, all of them emptying into the Gulf of Mexico, all of them able to accommodate salt-water traffic. The *Powhatan* could block one while the *Brooklyn* plugged another, but the other two remained open, and the Confederates were free to use them at will.

Porter wrote urgent requests to Captain McKean, off Mobile, and to the Navy Department in Washington, begging for reinforcements. He could slow the flow of traffic in and out of New Orleans, he said, and could make a nuisance of himself, but the blockade would be meaningless until he was given enough ships, guns, and men to seal off every delta channel.

The Navy was paying the penalty for its short-sighted refusal to build new ships, and Secretary Gideon Welles was forced to buy, rent, and commandeer every ship he could find. Two small steamers arrived to reinforce the blockade, and a new commander, Captain W. Mervine, was on board one of them. Porter promptly petitioned him for permission to send to Havana for spare parts and tools to repair the *Powhatan's* decrepit engines.

Late in June, a swift Confederate raider, the *Sumter*, slipped past the slow, awkward *Brooklyn* into the Gulf of Mexico to begin a career of harassing Union shipping, and newspapers throughout the North redoubled their demands for a larger, more powerful Navy. Porter advocated an attack, in force, on Confederate shipping anchored at New Orleans, believing in the principle of destroying the enemy's ability to wage war in a single, heavy blow. He sent a long, detailed memorandum to Captain Mervine, outlining his scheme. It was this notion, soon expanded, that led him to the idea of capturing New Orleans itself.

Meanwhile, early in July, he was temporarily distracted when he received a fatuous communication from Assistant Secretary of the Navy Gustavus Fox, who offered a promotion in rank to the first ship commander who captured a Confederate fort. Porter sent a blistering reply that was a masterpiece of restrained indignation. He would do his share of taking Confederate forts, he said, but their capture was irrelevant to his promotion, which was already five to eight years overdue. He and his men were suffering from heat, mosquitoes, and sand flies; when they went ashore for water they had to watch out for rattlesnakes and alligators. Their ships were decaying; they were on half-rations and eating rotting food, but their morale remained high, and they would take their due share of enemy forts. But neither he nor they would accept as "special rewards" what their labors had earned them.

His communication ended on an angry, impudent note. "Take this home," he wrote, "and read it Sunday night, when you have nothing better to do."

The anxiety of the blockaders increased when they heard rumors, soon substantiated, that a propeller-driven steamer was being sheathed in iron at New Orleans, and would be used as a moving battering ram to destroy the Union vessels conducting the blockade. Porter was relieved, during the second week in August, when he received the materials from Havana that enabled him to repair the *Powhatan*'s leaking boilers.

The ship was made seaworthy within forty-eight hours, and he immediately asked Mervine for permission to seek out and destroy the *Sumter*, which had captured nine Union merchantmen in recent weeks. Captain Mervine granted the request, even though it meant a serious weakening of the thin blockade line below New Orleans.

The wheezing *Powhatan* steamed down into the Caribbean shipping lanes, her problems compounded by the antagonism of officials in Cuba and Jamaica, Curaçao, Trinidad, and Martinique. The governments of Spain, Great Britain, and France were friendly to the Confederacy, he discovered, and only in the little town of St. Thomas in the Danish Virgin Islands did he receive a warm welcome and concrete information that might lead him to the elusive raider.

The *Powhatan* sailed as far south as Brazil, but in vain, and on his voyage northward, Porter again stopped at St. Thomas. There the captains of two other Union ships were refueling, and he learned from them that Captain McKean had replaced Captain Mervine in the delta of the Mississippi. He learned, too, that there had been a flurry of fighting at Pensacola. Still regarding Fort Pickens as his personal responsibility, he temporarily abandoned his search for the *Sumter* in order to investigate the situation in Florida.

The officers stationed at the fort greeted him as "Commander Porter." His long overdue promotion had materialized at last, spurred by his angry letter to Assistant Secretary Fox, and he was elated. But his joy was tempered by the failure of his attempt to find and sink the *Sumter*. Sailing off to join Captain McKean at the Mississippi delta, he was afraid the *Powhatan* was becoming too decrepit to be of value in battle. McKean's news was disturbing. A Confederate ironclad had sailed down the river from New Orleans, and had rammed two Union ships, damaging both. And a swift, agile Confederate gunboat had escaped into the Gulf to harass Union merchant shipping. There could be no doubt that, operating from a large, secure base, the Confederacy was winning the naval war in the Gulf of Mexico.

For the present, at least, Commander David Porter could no longer participate in that campaign. The *Powhatan* was in desperate need of a major overhaul, and McKean regretfully ordered his subordinate to take the limping ship to New York.

On the painfully slow voyage, Porter had ample opportunity to thoroughly review the situation and reached several important conclusions. The *Sumter* and the Confederate gunboat, the *Ivy*, were serious nuisances, as was the ironclad ram, *Manassas*, but all of these ships were symptoms rather than causes of the basic problem. The Gulf of Mexico would not become safe for Union shipping unless and until New Orleans was captured. And the Confederacy could not be dealt a death blow in the West until the Mississippi was sealed off, thus depriving her of incoming and outgoing trade on the great river.

Reaching the Brooklyn Navy Yard on November 9th, Porter had become convinced that his strategic concept was right, and was eager to persuade his superiors in Washington to adopt his point of view. No one could question the hard fact that the age of steam had replaced that of sail, and war at sea necessarily had to be fought according to scientific techniques. His pursuit of the *Sumter* had been old-fashioned and romantic; although he had enjoyed the experience, he knew that even had he found and sunk the raider, her place would have been taken by others. It was essential that the roots of the trouble be eliminated.

Georgy and the four children who were at home greeted David joyously, and Essex, accompanying his father, found an Army commission as a captain awaiting him. Carlisle, meanwhile, had become a midshipman at the Naval Academy, which had been moved to Newport, Rhode Island for the duration of the war.

A few hours after his arrival, Porter was closeted with Secretary Welles, Assistant Secretary Fox, and several members of the Senate Naval Affairs Committee. Using charts which he sketched as he spoke, Porter informed them that there were too many passes in the Mississippi delta to blockade New Orleans and cut off river traffic. The only way to accomplish the feat would be to capture New Orleans.

The Navy, he knew, was still suffering from a lack of enough powerful ships, but he believed this difficulty could be surmounted. His tactical scheme was simple. The Union's most effective weapon in the war, to date, had been the thirteen-inch mortar. So he suggested that mortars be mounted on a fleet of small schooners, large numbers of which had been used extensively in coastal merchant shipping. There was no shortage of them.

The schooners, he suggested, could subject the principal forts guarding New Orleans to an intense mortar bombardment for a period of at least forty-eight hours. The forts would be severely weakened, if not destroyed, and the moment the bombardment was lifted, the main Union fleet could race past these bastions to the city itself. Rendered defenseless, New Orleans would fall. And the isolated delta forts would be arms and legs cut off from the head — so they, too, would be compelled to surrender.

Welles and Fox were enthusiastic, as were the Senators, and the Secretary immediately took David to the White House. President Lincoln, who had known New Orleans since his youth, when he had made voyages down the Mississippi by flatboat, was impressed. He wanted an expert's professional opinion, however, and summoned General George B. McClellan, his new Army commander.

The cautious McClellan pointed out that Forts Jackson and St. Philip, below New Orleans, were among the strongest in all of North America. Both were equipped with heavy coast defense guns, mounted in tiers behind thick shields of stone, and could pound the wooden ships of the main Navy task force to kindling. Porter, at his impassioned rhetorical best, countered by insisting that the mortar bombardment, if sufficiently heavy, could drive the Confederate gunners in the forts from their battle posts long enough for the main fleet to slip past them.

Within twenty-four hours President Lincoln made one of the most vital strategic decisions of the war: Commander David Porter's plan would be adopted, and a major effort would be made to capture and occupy New Orleans.

Plans had to be made in the utmost secrecy, and Fox assumed the burden of assembling fourteen or fifteen of the Union's best steam-driven warships for the squadron that would run the gamut of the forts. Porter, summoned to the Assistant Secretary's office, was informed — unofficially at this juncture — that he would be given command of the unit that would become known as the mortar flotilla. His first tasks would be the ordering of mortars from foundaries in Pittsburgh and New England, the purchasing of schooners, and the building and installation of mortar carriages on their decks. He would also be responsible for assembling a dozen or more light steamers that would tow the mortar schooners up the Mississippi.

Obviously, he would need months to make his preparations. It was equally obvious that he soon would be promoted to the rank of captain.

The success or failure of the ambitious campaign would depend on the overall commander of the fleet, and Secretary

Welles conferred at length with the President on the subject. Their final choice was acting Commodore David G. Farragut, David's foster-brother and his late father's protégé. Although sixty years old, Farragut had all of the necessary qualifications for the post. He was a superb leader of men and a brilliant tactician, personally courageous, and, as a follower of the audacious Commodore Porter, a believer in attack as the best guarantee of victory.

Before the President made the appointment, however, Welles took the unusual step of consulting Porter, who was elated, and declared: "He is the best of all possible men for the post!"

One advantage of the appointment was self-evident: the fleet commander and the officer in charge of his mortar flotilla would be required to work in the closest coordination. Commodore Farragut and Commander Porter were not only closely related and had the greatest admiration for each other, but they thought alike in terms of waging war at sea.

One final step remained. The Secretary asked Porter to sound out his foster-brother to determine whether or not he wanted the post. Through a strange and happy coincidence, Commodore Farragut had just returned to Washington from sea duty, and was dining with his wife at the Porter house the following evening. The two men retired to David's cramped library immediately after dinner, and talked until dawn. When they finally emerged, both were smiling and neither appeared fatigued.

The President signed the necessary, secret orders, and the step-brothers went to work immediately. Porter sent requests to foundries in Pittsburgh and Worcester, Massachusetts, for twenty huge mortars, then quickly doubled the order. He also requested thirty thousand thirteen-inch shells. The foundries were already running far behind schedule, because of Army orders placed by General U. S. Grant, but Commander Porter was so persistent in his efforts that his requests received first consideration.

In December, 1861, and the first month of the following year, Porter worked sixteen to twenty hours daily, displaying an energy and devotion to detail that astonished Assistant Secretary Fox, who became his firm supporter and close friend. He visited a number of Union seaports, from New Haven to Baltimore, and personally selected his twenty mortar schooners, as well as the seven shallow-draft steamers and converted ferryboats that would comprise his mortar flotilla. He supervised the installation of mortar carriages in the schooners, and not only ordered but inspected the ammunition, food, naval stores, and medical supplies he would carry. He interviewed many officers, too, without telling them the nature of his mission, and was careful in the selection of his subordinates for the expedition. At home, late at night, he studied the records of enlisted men and requested the transfer to his force of the best gunners.

Somehow he also found time to perform a service for Fox, and visited the Navy Yards at Brooklyn, Philadelphia, and Mystic, Connecticut, in order to report on the progress of vessels under construction. On this journey he met John Ericsson, the inventor and ship designer, and inspected Ericsson's revolutionary ironclad, the *Monitor*, which, in the immediate future, would make wooden-hulled warships obsolete.

By early February the mortar schooners and most of the steamers had sailed for the rendezvous point, Key West. On February 11th Porter departed from the Washington Navy Yard on board his tiny flagship, the *Harriet Lane*, a former

Treasury revenue cutter. It was typical of him that, even when initiating the most important mission of his life, he interrupted his voyage long enough to capture a small Confederate merchantman that was trying to run the Union blockade.

Immediately after reaching Key West, late in February, he summoned the captains of his twenty mortar schooners to a council of war. Assigning them to three divisions, commanded by Lieutenants W. W. Queen, Watson Smith, and K. R. Breese, he ordered them to maneuver at sea, by divisions, from dawn until nightfall daily, and to practice their mortar gunnery by firing at barrels thrown overboard.

The key to their success, he explained to the lieutenants, after finally revealing their mission to them, would lie in a combination of speed, maneuverability, and pin-point gunnery. The mortar flotilla would become a unified, single, operational weapon, and would function according to the highest scientific standards that were possible to achieve.

Several experienced Coast Survey civilians had accompanied the ships to Key West, but Porter was not yet ready to explain why he had brought them on the voyage. It was sufficient, for the present, that they would make a significant contribution, playing an important role in the precise, farsighted plans he had made.

Discipline, he told the lieutenants, was essential, and he promised them he would tolerate no deviation from strict, instant obedience at all times. He quickly proved as good as his word, and in the next few days a number of officers and sailors, including two schooner captains, were relieved of their duties when they protested they were being forced to work too hard.

These unfortunates were put into irons at the small base that had been established in Key West, and were immediately replaced. Porter's planning had been so thorough that he had deliberately carried more officers and men than he needed, just so he would not be impeded by malcontents in an emergency.

One major worry nagged at him: four of his steamers had not arrived at the rendezvous. One of them, the *Miami*, finally appeared, reporting that it had encountered a vicious gale at sea, and Porter was afraid the others had been lost. He could not afford to wait for them, however. He and Commodore Farragut were operating on a tight schedule, and on March 6th he left Key West in the *Harriet Lane*, escorted by the *Miami* and the *Owasco*, to meet the commander in chief.

Farragut had reached Ship Island, off the town of Biloxi, Mississippi, on February 20th, and had relieved Commodore McKean. Wanting to keep the Confederates in the dark regarding the real nature of his intentions, he went through the motions of maintaining the blockade of the Confederate Gulf ports that his predecessor had already established.

In the following days his gunboats and some of his larger vessels gradually drew closer to Ship Island, and for the benefit of Confederate spies who might be in the area, the commodore let it be known that he was contemplating an attack on either Mobile or Galveston.

A raid on Biloxi, made on March 1st for the purpose of gathering information, produced unexpected results. Confederate newspapers taken by the raiders carried the news that General Grant and Navy Captain Andrew H. Foote, in a combined Army and Navy operation, had captured Forts Henry and Donelson on the Tennessee and Cumberland Rivers. Foote, commanding a flotilla of ironclad gunboats, was now moving down the Mississippi.

The Confederates were disorganized; all available warships were moving north to meet Foote; and even the ironclad battering ram, *Manassas*, had left her berth at New Orleans. Farragut realized that the sooner he attacked — while other pressures were being exerted on the enemy — the greater would be his chances of achieving the total victory that the President and Secretary Welles demanded.

Accordingly, on March 7th, without waiting for his mortar flotilla or the supply ships carrying his ammunition, coal, and hospital stores, the commodore moved to the Mississippi delta and began the arduous task of hauling his heavier ships over the mud bars into the main channel of the river below New Orleans.

The Confederates now knew his goal, but found it impossible to believe that wooden ships could survive a battering from Forts Jackson and St. Philip.

Porter, meanwhile, reached Ship Island on March 11th, and learned that one of his steamers had been lost. Since he could not replace the ship, he knew he would have to do his best without her. The schooners joined him under their own sail, the other steamers arrived, and the mortar flotilla moved on to the delta to join Commodore Farragut.

On March 18th the steamers began the task of hauling the mortar schooners over the mud bars. This task was completed with dispatch, and the flotilla's steamers were used for the far more difficult work of tugging the larger warships into the deeper channel of the Mississippi.

Every hour counted. The Confederates now realized that a major effort would be made to capture New Orleans. If they were given too much time to strengthen their forts, they could make their defense position virtually impregnable. Porter, personally supervising the operations of his six steamers, worked so furiously that even Farragut was afraid he might collapse, and told him that he must get more rest.

"I'll sleep," Porter replied, "after we've taken New Orleans."

VIII

PRESIDENT JEFFERSON DAVIS of the Confederacy had served with distinction as an officer in the United States Army in the Mexican War, and, eventually rising to the rank of full colonel, had given serious thought to the pursuit of a military career before politics had made a permanent claim on him. He still thought of himself as a military strategist, with good cause, and his estimate of the threat to New Orleans coincided with that of his high command.

The Confederates believed that the city's defense bastions, particularly Forts Jackson and St. Philip, were strong enough to drive off, and perhaps destroy, Farragut's fleet of wooden-hulled ships. Andrew Foote's ironclad gunboats on the Mississippi north of New Orleans constituted the real menace. For that reason most of the iron gunboats stationed at the city were sent north, and all troops that could be spared were transferred to the corps of the brilliant area commander, General P. G. T. Beauregard, who was bracing for another coordinated attack by Foote and Union General Ulysses S. Grant.

Farragut and Porter desperately needed every hour of each day to prepare for battle. The shallow water and mud of the delta channels were even greater obstacles than they had anticipated, and the moving of the commodore's large ships into the navigable waters of the Mississippi's mainstreamed proved to be a nightmare. A side-wheeler, the *Mississippi*, created the most serious problems. Four of Porter's steamers towed her, but her wheels dug into the soft mud, and she could not be moved more than a foot or two at a time.

Porter's patience was as inexhaustible as his energy, and, although the members of the commodore's staff urged him to abandon the project, he refused. Every ship would be needed, he said, and the *Mississippi's* guns were too powerful for her to be left behind. Setting the example for his subordinates, he worked more than twenty hours out of each twenty-four, ate his meals in the open while continuing to supervise the operation, and laughed when junior officers told him he would collapse if he didn't rest.

Finally, on April 4th, his herculean efforts were rewarded. After eleven days of incessant labor, the *Mississippi* reached deep water and was ready for combat.

By April 7th Commodore Farragut was ready to push past the Confederate forts. Every officer in his fleet knew that the task would tax their courage, skill, and stamina. The enemy had placed eight old schooners in the river as a barrier, lashing them together and trailing long chains and other obstacles from them to foul the propellers of the Union vessels.

Using the *Harriet Lane* as the flagship for his mortar flotilla of twenty-six vessels, Porter joined the fifteen large ships of the commodore's main fleet and then informed the senior officers there would be another delay. Having navigated the Mississippi many times as the master of a mail steamer, he knew the deep-water channel was narrow and that it constantly shifted, and his years of experience in the Coast Survey had taught him the urgent importance of precise charting.

He was prepared for the situation. The Coast Survey had loaned him its best steamer, the *Sachem*, and at his request its most competent civilian surveyor, F. H. Gerdes, had sailed from New York to join him. Porter now ordered Gerdes to prepare accurate maps of the channel as far upstream as the

Confederate forts, and the commodore provided the *Sachem* with an escort of two gunboats.

Confederate scouts, most of them excellent shots, were watching the movements of the Union fleet, and were bewildered by what they observed in the next few days. Small boats put out from the *Sachem*. Civilians went ashore and either drove markers into the soft ground on the banks or erected curious little weathervanes on the roofs of deserted houses. Although the Confederates had no idea what was happening, they tried to disrupt the activity with musket fire, but were driven off by retaliatory small cannon fire from the gunboats.

Porter was not content to remain with his own unit. He probably knew more about surveying than any other man in the United States, and on April 11, twenty-four hours after Gerdes had begun his task, Porter joined him and took an active part in the operation. They were hampered by two days of heavy rains and winds that swept down from the north, but refused to halt and wait for better weather. On April 14th Porter returned to the commodore's flagship, the *Hartford*, carrying accurate maps of the Mississippi's main channel.

Then the mortar flotilla sailed past the main fleet to take up a position near the west bank of the river, and on Wednesday, April 16th, three of the mortar schooners were towed to a position less than three thousand yards below Fort Jackson. His thirteen-inch mortar shells had a trajectory of 2,850 yards, and he was anxious to establish the range, precise fire being essential to the success of the overall operation. Several of Farragut's gunboats accompanied him, and remained in mid-channel in order to provide a diversion.

The Confederate reply was prompt and ingenious. A raft, piled high with dry pine logs smeared with pitch and resin, was set on fire and sent downstream with the tide, forcing the gunboats to scatter. According to several Union officers, flames shot at least a hundred feet into the air from the raft.

Several Confederate river steamers also sailed down the Mississippi to harass the invaders, and not until Friday, April 18th — Good Friday — was Porter ready to move his divisions into place. Lieutenant Watson Smith's unit was towed into position, and no sooner were the schooners anchored than they opened fire on Fort Jackson. Under this protective cover, the third division, commanded by Lieutenant K. Randolph Breese, was placed in position directly downstream from Smith's ships.

Lieutenant W. W. Queen's second division had the most difficult task — that of crossing the open river, where it was exposed to fire from both Fort Jackson and Fort St. Philip, its eventual target. The gunboat *Owasco* moved into midchannel to divert the enemy, and succeeded almost too well. After maneuvering incessantly for almost two hours and miraculously escaping, the *Owasco* appeared in danger of being blown from the water. Porter reluctantly ordered her to retire, while several other gunboats sailed upstream to take her place. By early afternoon, however, Queen's schooners were in position and opened fire and from the outset, the gunnery of the mortar batterymen was superb.

"A gunner in the United States Navy," Porter remarked a number of years later, "must be able to knock an enemy's teeth from his mouth, one by one. In the fight below New Orleans, my crews achieved the highest degree of accuracy any commander could desire."

Each mortar was fired every ten minutes. The roar was deafening, and the Confederates, responding instantly to the challenge, replied with heavy cannonading from the forts. Porter, supervising the operations of his flotilla, calmly had himself rowed from one schooner to another, ignoring the shot that fell into the river around him. He was on board Lieutenant Queen's lead schooner, the *T. A. Ward*, when a one-hundred-and-twenty-pound Confederate shell ripped off a portion of the schooner's cabin and smashed through her hull on the starboard side. Although his juniors were dismayed and fearful, he remained poised. When the next schooner in line, the *George Mangham*, sustained a hit a few minutes later, he calmly ordered both ships towed to new, less vulnerable positions.

At five o'clock in the afternoon, flames stabbed high into the air from Fort Jackson, and Porter sent a preliminary report to Commodore Farragut expressing the belief that he had put a number of fire rafts out of commission. Soon afterward, the guns of the fort fell silent, and at six o'clock the Union mortars were given a respite.

Porter was anxious to assess the results of the day's work and, although he could have sent any junior officer on a reconnaissance mission, he preferred to make his own judgments. Waiting until night had fallen, he had himself rowed upstream. Apparently he was indifferent to the possibility of being captured, killed, or injured.

He was surprised to see that his earlier assumption had been wrong, and that fires, raging in Fort Jackson's citadel and barracks, were causing extensive damage. While being rowed back to his flagship he brooded silently about his next step. His reflections resulted in the introduction of a new doctrine in naval warfare. For several thousand years the men of civilized nations had observed an unwritten code in combat at sea, and the principles of chivalry had been intensified during the Middle Ages, when the ideals of knighthood had become universal in the West. It was taken for granted that there would be a pause in battle from sundown until dawn the next morning, giving each side the opportunity to bury their dead, tend their wounded, and obtain a measure of rest before the next round began.

But the fires raging at Fort Jackson made David Porter realize that a victory could be achieved more rapidly, and with less loss of life on both sides, if the pressure on the Confederates was maintained without a respite. That night he conferred with Farragut, who gave unqualified approval to Porter's idea, and on Saturday, April 19th, a new chapter in the history of naval warfare was inaugurated.

Promptly at six o'clock in the morning the Union mortars resumed their bombardment. All through the day they maintained a steady, accurate fire. Several of the schooners were mauled by the Confederates, and Porter actually wrote in his log that he was afraid Fort Jackson was proving too strong for him. But he did not give up his new plan, and the mortars continued their bombardment through the long night.

On Easter Sunday, April 20th, a light rain fell, but the mortar fire did not slacken. A deserter from Fort Jackson told the Union officers that the parapets of the Fort were crumbling, sea walls were being breached, and fires were still raging. Porter and Farragut were encouraged, and the mortars continued to fire around the clock.

At one o'clock in the morning on Monday, April 21st, Fleet Captain H. H. Bell, Farragut's second-in-command, took three gunboats up the river under the cover of the mortar barrage, and succeeded in smashing the barrier of old schooners and chains that the enemy had thrown up across the Mississippi. Before dawn the Confederates replied by sending another fire raft down the river, and two Union vessels were damaged before the flames could be extinguished.

Tuesday, April 22nd, was the fifth day of the bombardment. The weary gunners were dazed, and no one in the flotilla, including Commander David Porter, had washed, changed his clothes, or eaten a hot meal since the fight had started. But the spirits of everyone in the unit remained astonishingly high. Around noon, Commodore Farragut came to the *Harriet Lane* to make an inspection, and told Porter that several British and French naval officers, whom he had allowed to pass through his lines for the purpose of communicating with their consulates in New Orleans, had returned a short time earlier, convinced that his wooden ships would be smashed to kindling by the fire from the forts.

"Sir," Porter said, "this uniform I'm wearing is a bit dirty at present, but it happens to be the best I own. I'll bet it against anything you care to wager that the fleet will reach New Orleans with a loss of no more than one ship!"

"I'd give a great many suits of new clothes to think and feel as you do," the commodore replied.

That night the senior officers of the fleet were summoned to the *Hartford* for a council of war during which Farragut informed them he intended to push past the forts before daybreak. Several asked for an additional twenty-four hours to make final preparations, however, and, because a strong, adverse wind from the north continued to blow, he finally agreed to wait until the following night. He made it clear to them, nevertheless, that he could delay no longer. The mortar flotilla was beginning to run short of ammunition, and General Mansfield Lovell, the Confederate commander of New Orleans' defenses, had finally become so alarmed that — according to Union spies — gunboats, cannon, and an ironclad ramming ship, the *Manassas*, had been recalled from Beauregard.

The mortars gave no indication that emergency reserves of shells were being used, and the unremitting bombardment continued at the same furious pace all through the day on April 23rd. Precisely at midnight, however, they abruptly terminated their fire. Then, in a daring maneuver that other senior officers considered suicidal, Porter silently sailed upstream and, protected by woods that grew down to the shoreline, anchored only two hundred yards from Fort Jackson's water battery — a line of low earthworks from which protruded the muzzles of the Confederates' most powerful cannon.

Porter had volunteered for the almost impossible task of neutralizing the water battery, even though its guns, and those of Fort St. Philip directly across the river, could blow every vessel of his unit out of the water. The schooners were silent and dark, awaiting the rest of the fleet.

At two o'clock on the morning of April 24th, Commodore Farragut's warships started up the Mississippi, the sloop *Cayuga* in the lead, followed by the frigate *Pensacola*.

The Confederates, who had been watching closely for the first major sign of enemy activity, immediately sent several fireships downstream and lighted huge bonfires on both banks of the river to aid their gunners.

Porter's mortars struck the first blows, opening fire on the water battery before the Confederate gunners could train their cannon on the Union ships. Within a few moments, however, the heavy artillery on both sides of the river came to life. The Union ships trying to run the gantlet opened fire with broadsides of their own, and the din was so great that many men were deafened for life by it.

Here was Porter's opportunity to demonstrate the devastating effect that massed firepower could have on a foe, and he made the most of it. Each mortar fired at intervals of only five minutes, and his gunners forgot their weariness, working with frenzied speed as they sent thirteen-inch shells screaming into the earthworks of the water battery.

Never had such concentrated naval fire been directed at a single target, but it was difficult to determine results in the inferno of exploding shells and dazzling bursts of light. Porter believed, but could not be certain, that some of the water battery's guns had been silenced.

The *Cayuga, Pensacola, Mississippi,* and *Oneida* got through safely as did four smaller Union ships directly in line behind them. But the Confederates were responding furiously. Tugs were guiding fire rafts downstream, and the ungainly *Manassas* churned down the river, a menace to anything in her path.

The tormented defenders of Fort Jackson were forced to divert their attention from the main Union fleet long enough to strike back at Porter's ships, and a screaming shell carried away part of the *Harriet Lane*'s superstructure. One sailor was killed and another badly wounded; both had been standing only a few feet from Porter, who miraculously escaped injury. He later noted in his log that other seamen immediately replaced those who were lost, and the nine-inch gun on his deck did not slacken its fire.

Commodore Farragut's flagship approached the forts, and the stately *Hartford*, with her towering masts and billowing sails, offered the Confederates their best target of the night. The guns of both forts blasted at her; the *Manassas* headed toward her on an erratic course intended to spoil the aim of Union gunners; and a fire raft, caught up by the swift current, unexpectedly bore down on her. The *Hartford* maneuvered wildly in an attempt to avoid the raft, and the flagship went aground directly in front of Fort St. Philip. At almost the same instant the raft spun into her, setting her entire port side on fire.

The crew of the *Hartford* responded to the emergency with disciplined vigor. A Confederate tugboat directing the raft was sunk; the fire was extinguished; and, while the gun crew exchanged broadsides at point-blank range with the Confederates in Fort St. Philip, the sailing crew managed to float the ship again. She resumed her drive up the river — battered, but proudly capable of moving under her own power.

The frigate *Brooklyn* took the worst beating of all the Union vessels. Her port anchor was caught in the remains of the hulks that had been used by the Confederates to block the river, and before she could disentangle herself, the land-based guns, particularly those at Fort St. Philip, pounded her mercilessly. Then, after she managed to free herself, the *Manassas*, which the *Hartford* had eluded, succeeded in ramming her. But the *Brooklyn* led a charmed life: recoiling from what was later interpreted as a glancing blow instead of a head-on crash, the frigate managed to make her way up the river.

The other major ships of the main fleet also passed the forts successfully, as did the smaller gunboats, with the exception of three — the *Pinola*, the *Winona*, and the *Itasca*. The coming of dawn made them perfect targets for the Confederate gunners in the forts with the consequence that they were forced to drift downstream again to await a more opportune moment.

The immediate mission of the mortar flotilla was ended. Porter ordered his ships to cease firing, and directed his steamers to withdraw from their exposed positions with all possible speed. The two Confederates forts were still standing, much to his disappointment, and from a distance appeared to be reasonably intact. Not until much later would he learn how much havoc he had wrought.

Shortly after sunrise, the ironclad *Manassas* drifted downstream, with smoke pouring out of several portholes. Curious about the unusual ship, Porter sent out a boat under a flag of truce to approach as closely as possible and report back to him any details that could be learned about the "pygmy monster," as the newspapers in the South had been calling her with affectionate humor.

The two junior officers in the boat quickly discovered that the supposed portholes were punctures in the armor of the *Manassas* that had been made by the shells of Commodore Farragut's fleet, and that she was no longer seaworthy. Several dazed members of her crew were taken off, and she drifted to the far side of the river, where she became stuck on a sandbar. Less than an hour later she exploded and sank. Thus the brief life of the only metal, steam-operated ramming ship in the history of naval warfare came to an abrupt end.

David Porter's position was extremely uncomfortable. He had no idea how many of Farragut's wooden ships had succeeded in running the gantlet, or what the final outcome of the battle had been. The evidence spread out before him was anything but reassuring: not only were a number of Fort Jackson's and Fort St. Philip's cannon still intact, but tied to the river bank above the latter was a Confederate ironclad warship, the *Louisiana*. Although not yet made seaworthy by her builders, she was being used as a floating, auxiliary fort, and her armor-plating was too thick to be pierced by the mortar flotilla's shells.

The uneasiness of the Union forces increased when several Confederate sailing ships came down the river to reinforce Fort Jackson and Fort St. Philip. No one knew whether they had participated in the previous night's action, but they appeared to be unscathed, which made it likely that they had been concealed in the deep bayous, or swamps, pending just such an emergency. With fresh crews and untapped ammunition supplies, they would be formidable opponents in battle.

But Porter, deciding he had everything to gain and nothing to lose, made a bold bid for peace, and sent an emissary to Fort Jackson under a flag of truce, demanding that the defenders surrender to him. Confederate General J. K. Duncan replied at once and, in terms equally polite and firm, refused.

The Union planners had not envisaged the situation that had developed, and Porter had no orders to cover the contingency. But he took matters into his own hands and resumed his mortar barrage, his guns firing so rapidly and steadily all day that the enemy had no way of guessing that his ammunition supplies were almost repleted. The Confederate response, particularly the fire from Fort Jackson, the key bastion, was so feeble, however, that Porter suspected he had done considerable damage and that General Duncan was suffering more than he cared to reveal.

At sundown the basic situation appeared unchanged. The Confederates remained adamant in their refusal to surrender, and the mortar schooners had used all but a few rounds of ammunition. Realizing that his ships, which had lost their principal weapons, were vulnerable to a night attack, Porter prudently withdrew down the river. There he placed them in a new formation, using his steamers to shield the mortar schooners.

Later that night a messenger dispatched by the commodore finally arrived with welcome news. Farragut had lost only one small ship and had suffered casualties slightly in excess of one hundred men killed and wounded — a remarkably low figure. The Confederates, on the other hand, had taken a severe beating. Eleven of their gunboats had been sunk or burned, and a full regiment of volunteer infantry, becoming panicky, had surrendered. The commodore was continuing his move up the river, confident that he would take New Orleans.

In the morning there was additional cheering news. General Benjamin F. Butler had landed in the delta region cleared by the Navy, and was marching north at the head of a strong Union corps of infantry, cavalry, and artillery. If necessary, he told Porter in a hastily scribbled note, he would take Fort Jackson from the rear.

There seemed to be little for Porter to do now but wait. He and Butler had cut off the forts to the south; Farragut's main fleet dominated the Mississippi to the north; and he believed the end for the enemy was both inevitable and near. Rather than risk additional, needless casualties on either side, he maintained a careful guard while resting on his arms.

On April 25th, soon after dark, the glow of huge fires could be seen up the Mississippi, leading both Confederate and Union troops to believe that New Orleans was burning. The following morning the hulk of a Confederate ironclad drifted down the river, still burning, and it was evident to the men on both sides that Farragut was winning his battle.

On Sunday, April 27th, General Butler's men went ashore from transports on both sides of the river and cut off escape from the rear of Fort Jackson and Fort St. Philip. Later that day a regiment of exhausted, frightened troops at Fort Jackson mutinied, and General Duncan knew the end had come. Two members of his personal staff rowed down the Mississippi under a flag of truce to the *Harriet Lane* for the purpose of informing Commander Porter that his surrender demand was accepted unconditionally.

The formal surrender took place on Monday, April 28th, at 2 P.M. Porter sailed up to Fort Jackson in his flagship, escorted by the gunboats that had been forced to remain downstream. General Duncan and his chief of staff came on board, and the articles of surrender were signed in the steamer's newly-repaired cabin. The ceremony was marred by the blowing up of the *Louisiana* whose commander preferred to destroy her rather than allow her to fall into Union hands. Porter immediately ordered that he and his subordinates responsible for the act be captured and, when apprehended, denied the usual privileges accorded prisoners of war.

The Confederate flag was lowered from the staff over Fort Jackson, and the Union banner was raised in its stead. One of the most gruelling battles in American history had come to an end. General Butler's troops marched into the forts to occupy them, and Porter moved up his mortar flotilla, anchoring off Fort Jackson. Then, to the dismay of his men, he ordered that all ships and guns be cleaned, that every member of his command bathe and wash his grimy clothes before they would be permitted ashore. No one dreamed of disobeying, and the Confederate prisoners were treated to the spectacle of Union sailors soaping their bodies and clothes in the water near the bank of the river.

On April 29th, an official courier appeared, carrying dispatches from the commodore to the Navy Department in Washington. New Orleans, Farragut said in a masterpiece of understatement, had fallen to him after a spirited fight. Included in his report were commendations citing the contributions to victory made by key members of his command, and at the head of the list was the name of Commander David Porter.

There was no need for the commodore to mention the obvious: the Confederacy had been deprived of her largest city, her most important port, and the key to her naval and commercial traffic. It was also self-evident that David Porter's theory of utilizing massed firepower in battle had been tried and proved to be successful.

Porter sent a brief personal letter via the courier to Assistant Secretary of the Navy Fox: "You good people at home can go to work now, cut down the Navy pay and disrate us to your hearts' content. My liver is turned upside down. My eyes are failing me, and I want to go to roost. But I'm not quite finished. One more slap at the Rebels — through Mobile — and I will be satisfied."

Even though one of the major engagements in naval history had just been concluded, and Porter had not yet slept in a bed or eaten a proper meal in days, he was already thinking ahead to the next round.

IX

UNION newspapers were filled with accounts of David Porter's accurate mortar fire in the Battle of New Orleans, and he was hailed throughout the North as a hero. But the praise meant as little to him as it did to Commodore Farragut, who had a number of relatives living in the city. Porter's attitude was similar to that of many professional officers; some of his closest friends, men with whom he had served for years, held commissions in the Confederate Navy, and the realization that they were the foes against whom his efforts were directed caused him grief that robbed him of the sense of accomplishment he otherwise would have felt.

Distressing personal news added to his unhappiness. A letter from Georgy told him that their son, Carlisle, who hated discipline and resented authority, had failed at the Naval Academy and had been dismissed. After brooding about the matter for several weeks, Porter finally wrote to Assistant Secretary Fox, asking that Carlisle be reinstated, if possible, provided the rules of the school weren't broken.

In a highly significant paragraph, he said, "He is a fine boy, and would make the right kind of officer, although he is not at present strong enough to meet the killing process which boys are subjected to at the Academy. I would ask nothing better after this war," he continued, unselfishly thinking in terms of keeping other high-spirited boys in the service, "than to have command of the Naval Academy, and get the right set of officers into the Navy. We don't want Miss Nancy's; we want fearless, dashing men."

The day when he could devote himself to peacetime pursuits was still far distant, however. Farragut ordered the mortar flotilla to lay siege to Mobile, and Porter undertook the task, which he privately considered boring. A ship bringing dispatches from Washington added to his restlessness. He was outraged, when reading accounts of the Battle of New Orleans, to discover that General Butler was claiming full credit for the victory. His anger and disgust destroyed the last vestiges of his respect for Butler. Although he did not realize it at the time, the news sparked a personal feud that would continue for many years and cause untold complications.

Then, in May, President Lincoln and his high command reached the conclusion that General Grant's efforts in the West would be of no avail if the Confederate troops under General Beauregard escaped across the Mississippi River into Arkansas and Texas. If this maneuver succeeded, the war might be prolonged indefinitely. Accordingly, the War and Navy Departments decided to force a showdown on the Mississippi, regardless of the cost. General Butler's corps was sent north from New Orleans, and Commodore Farragut was ordered to waste no time in placing the powerful Confederate port city and fortress of Vicksburg under blockade.

Farragut's larger ships could not sail up the shallow river, but the mortar flotilla was the perfect offensive weapon, and the commodore directed his foster-brother to proceed without delay to Vicksburg, four hundred miles up the Mississippi. Delays, however, proved inevitable. Below New Orleans, Porter spotted several Confederate tugs, which the Army had obtained as prizes. Since they would be valuable additions to his squadron, he asked Butler for them. The general was reluctant to part with them, but Porter was so insistent that Butler finally gave in.

A shortage of food supplies at New Orleans created problems, too, making it difficult to secure provisions for the mortar flotilla, and not until June 13th was Porter able to lead sixteen schooners, all hauled by tugs and other small steamships, in the direction of Vicksburg. The other four schooners left New Orleans a few days later, towed by Farragut's ships, which would push up the Mississippi as far as they could.

Porter wrote to Assistant Secretary Fox from his new flagship, the *Octorara*, that he was encountering difficulties greater than he had anticipated. He left New Orleans with the flotilla carrying half-ration, hoping to buy more food from farmers who lived along the river. But their storage bins were depleted, and the small quantities of food the plantation owners were willing and able to sell soon spoiled in the blazing June heat. Coal was running low, and swarms of mosquitoes attacked the sailors; the insects were carriers of malaria, although no one realized it, and many members of the expedition fell ill.

At the junction of the Red River and the Mississippi, Porter saw a number of flatboats he suspected might be carrying Confederate armaments, but he was under orders to reach his destination as rapidly as possible, so did not halt to make an investigation.

The bluffs on both banks of the Mississippi rose higher as the flotilla sailed northward, and from the heights Confederate scouts watched the progress of the enemy, sending up signal flares every night. Occasional shelling by small units of Confederate artillery did no damage, however, and on June 20th, seven days after leaving New Orleans, the flotilla completed its voyage. Porter ordered his ships to anchor well out of range of the Confederate batteries, but continued his own voyage northward in the *Octorara*, Wanting to learn all he could about the number of enemy guns at Vicksburg, their precise location, and their range, he deliberately sailed close to the fortress there, and shelled it. Typically, he made this dangerous reconnaissance mission himself rather than entrust it to a junior officer.

What he learned was not encouraging. Confederate General Mansfield Lovell had obtained heavy armaments for the defense of his post, and his cannon were emplaced in tiers, from the water's edge to the crests of hills rising more that two hundred and fifty feet from the bank of the Mississippi. The batteries, Porter informed Farragut, extended approximately fifteen hundred yards from the water, and the elevation was so great that the enemy guns would be difficult targets to hit.

Other problems arose to plague the flotilla. The survey ships had not accompanied the expedition, so the mortar schooners were berthed by a process of trial and error — a long, arduous, and exasperating task. The heat was so great that men were prostrated by it, and Porter was compelled to have the work done at night. Nine schooners were placed on the eastern bank of the Mississippi, under the command of Lieutenant Watson Smith, and were protected by overhanging trees; the other division, on the western bank, was placed under the command of Lieutenant Queen.

Commodore Farragut, in a daring and delicate sailing operation, arrived with three of his larger ships, the *Hartford*, *Brooklyn*, and *Richmond*, together with seven smaller gunboats. The commodore decided to employ the same technique that had been used below New Orleans, and on the night of June 25th the mortar flotilla opened its murderously accurate bombardment. Porter's guns, however, were only partly effective in striking targets high on the bluffs.

On the night of June 28th, the commodore's ten ships ran the gantlet successfully, but three of the smaller gunboats were severely damaged. A junction was made with Union ships farther up the river, demonstrating that the Union Navy — in theory, at least — could control the entire Mississippi. Porter, however, shared the commodore's feeling of discouragement.

Two of the mortar flotilla's steamships had sustained direct hits, and had suffered twenty-two casualties in killed and wounded. Moreover, the Confederates still held Vicksburg; the Union sailors were on starvation rations; and approximately one man out of three was prostrated by either heat or malaria. Until and unless Washington decided otherwise, however, there could be no lessening of the attack, and the bombardment continued until July 9th. Porter and Farragut both believed they were wasting their time, that Vicksburg could not be reduced by a naval attack alone. The Confederate forces there were too strong for Butler to attack, and the situation was made painfully clear in a long telegraphic report that Farragut sent to the Navy Department on July 4th.

On the night of July 9th, Washington telegraphed Farragut to break off the engagement and send the mortar flotilla to Hampton Roads in Virginia. The inconclusive fight came to an end, and Porter led his battered squadron back down the Mississippi. One significant incident took place on the voyage: a Confederate ship, the *Webb*, was seen at the junction of the Red River. It retreated, and was chased in vain for ten miles by one of Porter's steamers, convincing him that the Mississippi would not be truly safe for Union shipping until enemy resistance was halted on its tributary, the Red River.

While the flotilla sailed through the Gulf of Mexico into the open Atlantic and headed northward, the success the Navy had achieved at New Orleans finally brought encouraging results from Congress. Increased appropriations were voted, after long, futile efforts that had discouraged all but the Navy's most optimistic friends. A new, vastly expanded ship-building program was inaugurated. As a result of the Union's *Monitor* having defeated the Confederacy's *Merrimac* in a "duel of the ironclads," most of the new vessels would boast metal hulls. Bureaus of Navigation and Ordnance were established; a program of large-scale recruiting and training was inaugurated; and the new rank of rear admiral was created. The first officer promoted to that rank was David Farragut.

On July 26th the flotilla reached Norfolk, which the Confederates had evacuated after the *Monitor*'s victory. Porter, who had fallen ill with what was known as "intermittent fever," a relatively mild form of malaria, remained in bed until July 28th, and then hurried to Washington, where he reported to Secretary Welles and Assistant Secretary Fox. It was obvious that he was still ill, and should not have left his bed; he was therefore granted a leave of absence to join Georgy and the children who had gone to Newport in order to escape Washington's summer heat.

Porter was on the verge of collapse by the time he reached Newport. Concerned about his health, Georgy ordered him to bed. She kept him there for three days by reading newspapers to him, and by August 2nd he was well enough to visit the Newport Club, where Navy officers stationed at the local base congregated. There, renewing old friendships, he was free in his criticism of General George McClellan's Army of the Potomac, declaring that its lack of success was due to the general's failure to establish discipline in the ranks.

According to an old tradition, Navy and Army officers on active duty did not criticize colleagues in either service, but David Porter was his father's son and spoke his mind, indifferent to the consequences. In this instance his intemperate words caused a severe reaction, as he discovered when his leave ended and he returned to Washington in mid-August. His comments had been duly reported, and Secretary Welles had not only given his flotilla to another officer, but had also assigned the James River Flotilla, another choice command, to someone else. Assistant Secretary Fox told Porter he would be sent to Cincinnati to facilitate the building of new gunboats, a dreary post for an officer who craved action and had demonstrated his talent for combat.

Secretary Welles was holding a meeting in his office and could not be disturbed, so Porter, upset by the turn of events, requested permission to return to Newport on extended leave. Fox agreed. Porter left the Navy Department, but instead of going to the railroad station, hurried to the White House.

President Lincoln granted him an interview, heard his account of all that had happened on the Mississippi and, for the first time, learned that the Confederates intended to hold Vicksburg, no matter what the cost. Lincoln, a superb listener, made no comment when his visitor begged for an active command.

Porter returned to Newport, hoping the President would make some move on his behalf. He received no word of any kind from the Navy, however, and the next month was a torment. Furthermore, the exploits of his estranged brother, William D. Porter, now a commodore, aroused his jealousy and compounded his unhappiness: William, commanding the Union ironclad, *Essex*, had fought and destroyed the Confederate ironclad, *Arkansas*, in a spectacular battle.

Georgy was the only member of the Newport household who was not immersed in gloom. She was sorry her husband was suffering, but secretly rejoiced because the extension of his leave gave him the opportunity to recover his health. Porter rid himself of the fever, slept well, and regained his appetite. By late September, when the Navy called him to Washington for the purpose of receiving his new assignment, he was again the David Porter who had formed and led the famous mortar flotilla.

Secretary Welles and Assistant Secretary Fox had a stunning surprise waiting for him. At the direct order of the President, Porter was given command of the entire Mississippi Squadron, with the rank of acting rear admiral. Not only was he being raised over the heads of scores of senior officers but he was completely skipping the rank of captain. The promotion was completely without precedent.

On October 1st, after spending a week studying the Navy's confidential files, Porter went to the White House with the Secretary and Assistant Secretary. There, after he had thanked the President, he learned the scope of his mission. In cooperation with General John A. McClernand, one of U. S. Grant's principal subordinates, he was ordered to capture Vicksburg.

Before leaving Washington the same day for Cairo, Illinois, where he would assume his command, Porter wrote a hasty, jubilant note to his mother. "How proud my old father would be if he could see me an admiral," he wrote. "Yet it gives me pain to be hoisted over the heads of those old veterans who have so long considered the Navy as belonging to them. It seems somewhat like the Justice of Providence who takes this method of mortifying them for their treatment of my father."

The military fronts were temporarily quiet when Porter reached the little village of Cairo. There he learned that Grant and McClernand were in the field, resting and regrouping their forces, and that General William T. Sherman waited at

Memphis with still another corps. All were planning to move against Vicksburg.

The ships of the Mississippi Squadron were not awe-inspiring. Three river side-wheelers formed the nucleus of the flotilla. Although the *Lexington*, the *Tyler*, and the *Conestoga* were large, easy to maneuver, and carried heavy armaments, Porter knew at a glance that the Confederate forts could pound them to kindling. Seven unusual ironclads that had been designed and built for river service, with flat bottoms, and paddle wheels mounted in their sterns, had already proved their worth in combat. The fleet also included the new *Essex*, an ironclad ferryboat with a steam engine, and the *Benton*, also an ironclad with paddle wheels — the largest ship afloat on the Mississippi. A number of smaller vessels had also been accumulated, among them two hospital ships, supply boats and tugboats, ammunition boats, and several light sloops that would be utilized as dispatch boats. At the bottom of the list were small barges used for hauling coal, food, and ammunition, and several enormous barges that carried machinery used to repair steam engines and the hulls of ironclads.

Other ships for the squadron were being completed at yards in Cincinnati and St. Louis, and Porter hoped they would be ready for service by the time he moved against the foe. Meanwhile, a monumental task of reorganization awaited the new admiral. At his insistence, the squadron was being manned, in the main, by veteran sailors; these men were replacing Army conscripts, who, knowing nothing about ships, had reduced the efficiency of the units to which the vessels had been attached.

At Porter's request, Lieutenant K. R. Breese, one of his division chiefs in the mortar flotilla, was given a temporary promotion and became his fleet captain, a post later to be known as chief of staff. Captain Henry Walke, commander of the ironclad, *Carondelet* and related to Admiral Farragut, was an audacious officer with a quick mind, and Porter, striking an immediate rapport with him, made him the squadron's operations officer. Captain A. M. Pennock, commandant of the Naval Station at Cairo, was an old friend and could be depended upon for supplies and replacements.

The men of the squadron were instantly aware that a professional sailor had taken command. Discipline was tightened, and new precautions were taken to ensure the good health of the crew. Larger guns were installed on the ironclads. The ammunition barges hauled shells and powder to the ships night and day, and a tight security guard was established to prevent raids by Confederate guerrillas.

Porter also busied himself buying as many light, shallow-draft river steamers as he could find. He spent money with such abandon that Secretary Welles became alarmed, even though he had authorized the expenditures. Intent on forming and equipping a force that would overcome the enemy, Porter replied with polite evasiveness to each letter of protest — and continued to buy, arm, and staff the steamers.

By mid-November the squadron was ready to move. No word had come from McClernand, however, and Porter, becoming impatient, wrote to both Grant and Sherman, offering assistance. Early in December, General Grant arrived unexpectedly in Cairo, and Porter went into conference with him behind closed doors. Both men were wary at first, but each recognized the competent, professional approach of the other, and they soon reached an agreement. Grant said he and Sherman were ready to march on Vicksburg, and Porter enthusiastically agreed to attack the Confederate fortress from the river.

He quickly ordered all available vessels to make ready for action, and a vanguard was sent ahead under the command of Captain Walke. Since Porter did not feel at home on board the huge *Benton*, he designated the converted river steamer, *Black Hawk*, which had been given a metal-plated hull, as his own flagship.

On December 8th Grant and Sherman, who had just met at Oxford, Mississippi, decided not to wait for McClernand, whose failure to take the field was annoying. According to the newest plan, Grant would attack Vicksburg from the rear, while Sherman, returning to Memphis, would coordinate his march down the banks of the Mississippi with the movements of Admiral Porter's squadron.

A telegram was sent to Porter, who wired his immediate agreement, and on December 14th he left Cairo with the bulk of his fleet. He was so anxious to face the enemy with the strongest possible force that some of his ships were badly undermanned and others took part in the enterprise even though armed with only a single cannon.

En route to Memphis he learned of the campaign's first casualty. The *Cairo*, one of the squadron's initial seven ironclads, had been sunk by a Confederate torpedo in the Yazoo River, a Mississippi tributary. Instead of ordering a court of inquiry to look into the matter — hitherto a standard procedure — he declared, "I have no time to order courts. I can't blame any officer who seeks to put his ship close to the enemy!" Ordering Captain Breese to give the commander of the *Cairo* one of the large side-wheelers, he immediately succeeded in driving home the point to all captains in the squadron that audacity would be rewarded.

Porter and the equally hard-headed Sherman met at Memphis on December 18th, and agreed that they would try to reach Vicksburg by Christmas. Their schedule was optimistic, and speed was essential.

The *Black Hawk* left Memphis early on the morning of December 20th, and another precedent was smashed. The admiral's flagship, instead of taking a safe place in the line, acted as the vanguard for the squadron and the hundreds of Army transports it escorted.

Sailing rapidly with several of his more heavily armed ships, Porter arrived at the mouth of the Yazoo, eight miles north of Vicksburg, on December 24th. The heavy ironclads had cleared the tributary's mouth of torpedoes, and moved upstream slowly, continuing to dredge the Yazoo. Sherman's corps arrived at the mouth of the tributary late on Christmas Day, and the following morning Porter and the general made a personal reconnaissance of the surrounding countryside on horseback.

They decided to move the Army up the Yazoo to a swamp called Chickasaw Bayou, where the troops would disembark, then march against a line of hills, known as Chickasaw Bluffs, which guarded Vicksburg. This operation was carried out on December 27th, the squadron's ironclads exchanging heavy artillery fire with the Confederate batteries stationed on the heights.

The two forces maneuvered for thirty-six hours, and on December 29th Sherman began his main assault. Porter rendered considerable artillery support, although the range was great. He sent a dispatch boat to Memphis with a demand that all available mortar schooners be sent downstream immediately.

Meanwhile, Sherman was encountering great difficulties. A heavy rain fell, hampering his operation, and the ammunition boat, *Blue Wing*, had failed to arrive, resulting in a shortage of powder and shells. Chickasaw Bluffs remained in Confederate hands; the Union corps suffered severe losses; and the situation looked bleak. A further problem was the fact that Vicksburg had been heavily reinforced, and both Porter and Sherman realized that strenuous efforts would be needed to regain the initiative. No one knew how General Grant was faring in his attack on Vicksburg's rear. And, to complicate matters, General McClernand arrived on January 1, 1863.

A former lawyer, newspaper editor, and for ten years a member of Congress, McClernand was known as a "political" general, and Sherman was furious when he discovered that the newcomer carried orders giving him the command of the corps. Porter, who had struck up a close friendship with Sherman, shared his anger. Sherman, now reduced to the command of a wing, tried to deal with his new superior diplomatically. Porter, however, was openly rude to McClernand and told him flatly he would cooperate only in enterprises that Sherman commanded.

The squadron backed out of the Yazoo, and a new expedition was undertaken. Hoping to retrieve some measure of the honor he had lost at Chickasaw Bluffs, Sherman decided to try and capture a major Confederate outpost on the White River, sixty miles above the mouth of the Arkansas River and a little more than a hundred miles from Little Rock. If he could take the place, Vicksburg would be denied a major source of its supplies.

The combined forces of Sherman and Porter were overwhelming, and on January 11th, after a brisk battle, the Confederates at the White River outpost surrendered. McClernand, who had accompanied the expedition, accepted the sword of the Confederate commander, and his dispatches to the War Department made it appear that he had been the victor. Congress expressed its thanks to him, and, for the second time, officially congratulated Porter. His pleasure, however, was muted by the realization that the operation had been minor, and he could not share the opinion of McClernand and Congress that any real triumph had been achieved.

Meanwhile, the Confederates, still holding Vicksburg, were digging in there. And General Grant sent a scathing telegram to McClernand, rebuking him for going on a "wild goose chase" into Arkansas.

Grant, the overall Army commander in the West, joined his subordinates on January 18th. He had not yet committed his own troops, and intended to reorganize the subordinate command first. After listening to Porter, with whom he conferred privately, and then talking at some length with Sherman, Grant decided to amalgamate his forces. He gave Sherman the command of one corps and made McClernand the commander of another, thus placing them on the same level. The entire Army of the Tennessee, as his force was known, would made an attack on Vicksburg from the river side. Acting Rear Admiral David Porter gravely consented to give his full cooperation.

On January 18th the Mississippi Squadron was assembled in full strength at the mouth of the Yazoo, above Vicksburg. Porter's flagship became the temporary headquarters of the combined commands, with Grant and his subordinates coming there for daily conferences. After an exhaustive study of the situation, it was decided that the Army would have to be ferried to a point south of Vicksburg, running the gantlet of the Confederate cannon there. It would then disembark and approach the city from the south, where the hills were less rugged. But this operation would have to wait until the

Mississippi — now at flood crest — subsided somewhat, since an area stretching far inland had been turned into impassable swamps.

In the meantime, partly to keep their men occupied and maintain their spirits, Grant and Porter ordered a series of probing expeditions that would keep the enemy off balance and might, if highly successful, turn the Confederate flanks. For weeks the gunboats and General Sherman's corps sailed up swollen tributaries of the Mississippi, poked into bayous and swamps, and maintained lively exchanges with the Confederates.

"The men of the fresh-water Navy," Porter wrote to Assistant Secretary Fox, "are becoming water-rats. Spirits remain high, although life in the swamps leaves much to be desired. I am encouraged, and think the future is bright. Crewmen are learning to work together, and when the test comes, they will not be found wanting."

The overall operation Porter supervised was vast and complicated. In addition to the divisions supporting Sherman's corps, and other Army units conducting reconnaissance and engaging in skirmishes, the squadron's gunboats patrolled the Mississippi from Vicksburg to Cairo, keeping the river clear of guerrillas. When ice on the Ohio River melted, the patrol was extended from Cairo to Pittsburgh. Porter maintained pressure on the manufacturers of new ironclads at St. Louis and Cincinnati, bombarding them with letters that urged haste in delivery. He also dealt with them indirectly through the Navy Department in Washington, and, ultimately, dispatched officers to both cities for the purpose of improving the delivery deadlines.

Repair facilities at the Memphis and Cairo yards were expanded under his direction; his recruiting agents toured the

Union; and men who enlisted were put through a training program he devised, most of them stationed at Cairo for the purpose. His supply masters were busy scouring every state that bordered on the Mississippi and Ohio for provisions. Men who fell ill or suffered wounds were sent back to Memphis or Cairo for treatment and recuperation. Never had the United States known such a far-flung, superbly organized naval operation.

On March 22nd, while Porter was accompanying one of the gunboat divisions into the bayous on an expedition designed to harass the Confederate defenders, he received an urgent message from Fleet Captain Breese. Admiral Farragut, Breese reported, had sailed up the Mississippi from New Orleans, and was poised below Vicksburg. A division of gunboats and shallow-draft paddle-wheelers, led by several of the squat ironclads known as rams, had tried to sail south past Vicksburg to meet Admiral Farragut, and one of the rams, the *Switzerland*, had been sunk by Confederate guns. The rest of the division, consequently, had been forced to turn back.

Porter hurriedly left the swamps and rejoined his main command at the mouth of the Yazoo. The time for major action was at hand.

X

A SMALL river sloop carrying Admiral Farragut's son, Loyall, managed to evade the Confederate guns on the Vicksburg heights, and awaited Porter at his headquarters. Learning from young Lieutenant Farragut that the senior admiral's fleet was badly in need of provisions, Porter immediately sent off several large barges loaded with food, including a personal gift to the admiral of butter, cream, and fresh meat. The barges were floated down the Mississippi after dark, and, by hugging the shore on the bank opposite Vicksburg, managed to reach Admiral Farragut safely.

On March 26th, while preparing for the start of major operations, Porter sent his foster-brother a letter: "I intended to get over to see you, but General Grant says that it is a very long walk. I have been so much confined to the ship since I have been here that I have almost lost the use of my legs... Your son got over here safe, and I took him in. I expect he will give you an amusing account of my ménage. The first evening he came we had eight dogs in the cabin. Loyall was quite at home on mush and cream and fresh butter, all of which we have here in abundance."

Turning to more professional matters, Porter expressed his pleasure that Farragut had been able to raise and repair the *Switzerland*. He turned over the ram to his foster-brother's command, and suggested that he keep a sharp eye on her commander, "or he will go off on a cruise somewhere before you know it, and then get the ship into trouble. She is a very formidable ship as a ram, but I would never expect to see her again if she got out of your sight."

The letter was dispatched by river sloop that evening, and reached Farragut safely. The following evening his son returned, carrying with him an important message from Acting Rear Admiral Porter, which he had been instructed to destroy in the event he fell into the hands of the enemy. Porter had learned from the younger Farragut that the main fleet intended to block the mouth of the Red River, a major Mississippi tributary to the south, and he expressed strong approval of the pending operation.

"It will be an object for you to remain at the Red River as long as possible," Porter wrote, "and I hope you will do so. It is death to these Confederate people. They get all their grub from there, and we will be able to starve them out of Vicksburg (if we cannot drive them out) should you be able to dry up their sources of supply."

The following morning Farragut sailed off to blockade the Red River, and the foster-brothers did not meet. Thereafter, Porter increased the pace of his preparations for the major campaign that was about to start, and General Grant sent McClernand's corps to a point thirty miles below Vicksburg.

Porter continued to buy steamers, add iron hulls to every wooden ship, wheedle more cannon from Washington, and lash logs to his steamers at the water line in order to protect them from enemy shot. By mid-April both the Navy and Army were ready to begin the long-delayed, concentrated attack on Vicksburg. Porter's operation was so complex that he needed a large staff to handle the coordination of details, and reluctantly transferred his flag to the *Benton*, the largest vessel in his command. He was somewhat mollified by the thought that she carried more cannon than any of the other vessels.

Captain Walke wanted to lead the line that would sweep down the river past Vicksburg, and argued that his new ironclad, the *Lafayette*, was the perfect ship for the purpose. Porter, however, defying tradition as he had in the past, insisted that the *Benton* lead the procession, and Walke had to be content with following in second place.

At 8:45 P.M. on April 16th, Admiral Porter and his staff went on board the *Benton*, signalling the imminent start of the operation. A quarter of an hour later, lanterns were lighted, sending word to the ships in line at the mouth of the Yazoo that the expedition was getting under way. The squadron headed for the western bank of the Mississippi, and fifty thousand of General Grant's troops watched as the ships silently drifted down the river. Engine fires were lighted, making the engines ready for immediate use, but, for the present, Porter had ordered that his vessels use the current wherever possible in order to minimize noise.

At 10:30, when the lights of Vicksburg became visible through the tree branches, the order was given to start all engines. Confederate sentinels fired their muskets, giving the alarm, and tar barrels along the waterfront were set on fire to make the Union ships more plainly visible to the artillerymen on the heights. At 10:40, Admiral Porter's flagship swept around a bend and stood opposite Vicksburg. The element of surprise had been maintained until the last possible moment, but the Confederates had kept a sharp vigil, and the guns on the cliffs began to roar.

The *Benton* replied without delay. Her mortars and some of her larger cannon, which had been elevated, fired at the batteries on the cliffs. Her medium-sized guns fired at the city itself, and her smaller cannon were loaded with "grape" — small chunks of metal that were fired at the outposts on the shoreline.

Porter's gunners were the best in the squadron, and lived up to their reputation. In less than one minute they started a major fire in Vicksburg, and the glare of the flames, which mounted rapidly and steadily, made the city a better target for the Union cannoneers. But the *Benton* did not escape unscathed; a single shot tore through her armor-plating, which was two and a half inches thick, and wounded several sailors, two of them sustaining serious injuries.

Meanwhile, the other ships of the squadron were moving around the bend and adding their fire to the din. The Confederates kept up a steady stream of fire, too, but the ironclads and rams managed to run the gantlet unscathed. Two of the Union transports, which were loaded with supplies, were less fortunate. A Confederate shot set fire to bundles of hay, intended for use as fodder, on the deck of the *Henry Clay*, and the flames spread so rapidly that the vessel had to be abandoned. Another transport, the *Mirage*, ran aground on the western bank when she was inadvertently nudged by an ironclad, whose captain was unable to see her because of the smoke. An easy target for the Confederates because she could not be moved, the *Mirage* was severely pounded. When she, too, was set on fire, her crew abandoned her.

By 2:10 A.M. on the morning of April 17th the entire squadron had succeeded in running the gantlet. At daylight Porter led his ships down to New Carthage, Louisiana, and there his armorers and carpenters went to work repairing the battle damage. Except for the two lost transports the squadron was intact, and casualties had been low. Miraculously, no one had been killed, and only twelve sailors had suffered serious injuries.

The Army followed the Navy down the river at a slower pace, and, in late April, Porter met the military high command

149

at Grand Gulf, Mississippi, forty miles below Vicksburg. General Grant had intended to cross the river there, but the Confederates had recognized the importance of the easily-defended point, and had erected numerous new artillery fortifications there. It was necessary to reduce these batteries, and Porter believed this was a task for the Navy.

On the morning of April 29th, at 8:00 o'clock, he led his ironclads in an attack on the fortifications. The battle lasted until early afternoon and was one of the most vicious engagements of the entire war. The squadron won the upper hand, although the Confederates were not driven out of their strongholds, and Porter paid heavily for his partial victory. Every one of his ironclads sustained damage. Twenty-four of his men were killed — half of them officers — and fifty-six were severely injured. Porter himself suffered a slight wound when a shell burst above the *Benton*'s upper deck and he was struck by a small flying splinter. He refused medical treatment, however, and remained at his post.

General Grant cautiously insisted on moving still farther south, and finally, between April 30th and May 3rd, Porter ferried the Army of the Tennessee across the river for what proved to be the climactic phase of Grant's epic campaign against Vicksburg. The Army commander estimated he would need at least two weeks to move his forces into position for the final strike. When that time arrived, he wanted the further help of the squadron, but until then had no further need of Navy assistance.

Porter had no intention of allowing his powerful force to remain idle for that length of time. His gunboats were better able to maneuver up the Red River than were the larger vessels of Farragut's fleet, so he sailed to join his foster-brother, intending to augment his forces and, if Farragut wished, relieve him of blockade duty.

Farragut was delighted to be relieved, explaining that he was badly needed in New Orleans. His basic assignment was to keep the entire Gulf of Mexico clear of Confederate shipping, a task that required his full attention. He withdrew his larger ships, which were unable to proceed beyond the mouth of the Red River and transferred the ironclad gunboat, *Arizona*, to the Mississippi Squadron. Returning to New Orleans, he carried a request from Porter to General N. P. Banks, commander of the Union garrison there, asking him to send a task force to Alexandria, Louisiana, as quickly as possible.

Wasting no time himself, Porter moved up the Red River, deep into Louisiana. He encountered none of the enemy until he reached Fort de Russy, sixty miles upstream, which the Confederates were just building. His ironclads smashed through a barrier of chains and logs, and the Confederates fled. Forging on, the squadron sailed fifteen miles farther up the river to the town of Alexandria, where he discovered that the enemy had retreated to Shreveport.

General Banks reached Alexandria twenty-four hours after the squadron had raised the Union flag, and Porter turned the town over to him. As the Red River was too shallow above Alexandria for the gunboats, Porter sent a small force in converted river steamers to find and destroy two Confederate river raiders — the *Queen* and the *Webb* — which had done considerable damage to Union shipping. The task force was unable to locate the vessels, but either confiscated or burned provisions worth at least $500,000 that were found piled high at boat landings. These stores consisted of bacon, salt, sugar, and molasses.

Returning to Fort de Russy, Porter leveled the enemy fortifications there. Then, after leaving a division on the Red River under Captain Walke's command, he sailed back to the Mississippi. Fleet Captain Breese had done well during his absence, intermittently shelling Vicksburg, transferring Sherman's corps to the eastern bank of the river, and maintaining a constant vigil on the Mississippi. One more transport had been lost to enemy gunners. Meanwhile, Grant had succeeded in driving a wedge deep between the forces of Confederate Generals Joseph E. Johnston and John C. Pemberton.

New ironclads from Cincinnati and St. Louis were joining the squadron under crews trained at Cairo, and while Porter integrated them into his command, Grant forced Pemberton's Confederates to retreat into Vicksburg. Miles of fortifications on the Yazoo River were evacuated, and Porter promptly ordered his ships to destroy them. Guns were spiked; entrenchments were smashed; and one task force pushed fifty miles up the Yazoo, burning an entire Confederate naval yard to the ground. Another smaller force cleared tributary rivers of Confederate installations, burning all provisions.

The mortar ships that had won renown for Porter were moved into position above Vicksburg and fired their shells into the besieged city, day and night. Meanwhile, the squadron doubled its vigil on the Mississippi to prevent the enemy from escaping across the river. Pressure from Grant behind the city mounted as June wore on, and the mortars on the water continued their unrelenting bombardment.

On July 3rd Grant sent Porter a message, asking him to cease firing until notified otherwise, the Confederates having asked for an armistice. The shelling was not resumed. At 11:30 A.M. on Independence Day the Confederate flag was lowered and the Stars and Stripes were raised above Vicksburg. The most important Confederate bastion other than Richmond, the capital, had fallen.

Porter immediately sent his fastest dispatch boat up the Mississippi to Cairo with a telegram to Secretary Welles in Washington. His flag secretary, Charles Gould, left at once for Washington, carrying a full account of the siege's end. Shortly after noon, General Grant came on board the *Black Hawk*, which Porter was again using as his flagship. The victorious general and acting rear admiral exchanged congratulations, and Porter gave orders to open the wine he had saved for the occasion.

Secretary Welles received Porter's message on the afternoon of July 7th — the first word to reach Washington that Vicksburg had been taken. Welles hurried to the White House with the news, and an elated President Lincoln made Porter's promotion to the rank of rear admiral permanent, jumping him three ranks.

The entire Mississippi was now in Union hands. Not only could the North use the vital waterway for both commercial and military traffic without fear of disruption, but the Confederacy was cut in two, her territory west of the great river having been isolated. The Union celebrated its greatest victory, and the nation acknowledged Grant and Porter as heroes. The general and the newly-promoted admiral generously gave each other full credit, both publicly and privately. Thus an important personal friendship had been forged in battle.

In the autumn of 1863, the squadron's shallow-draft vessels accompanied Grant on his Chattanooga campaign, and kept his lines of communication open on the Tennessee and Cumberland Rivers. Meanwhile, Porter returned to Cairo, where he made his headquarters. His divisions patrolled the Mississippi; damaged ships were repaired; and the canny admiral took advantage of his hero's status to insist that new shallow-draft ironclads, monitors, and rams be built for him, all of them heavily armed with cannon. He knew what lay ahead for his command — as did his friends, Grant and Sherman — although no civilian could as yet guess what the future might hold. In any event, Secretary Welles approved of the new shipbuilding request, and a grateful Congress provided the funds.

While at Cairo Porter enjoyed a visit from his mother, who was returning home after visiting friends in Missouri. Evalina Porter was in excellent health, but was deeply concerned about her estranged eldest son. William, who was slowly dying in New York, had been suspended from duty on charge of insubordination brought against him by Admirals Farragut and C. H. Davis, and was not helping his cause by defending himself in vehemently angry interviews he gave to the press.

During a visit to Cincinnati early in the winter to inspect the new ironclads being built there, Porter caught a severe cold that lingered through the winter. In spite of his poor health he insisted on riding horseback at least an hour each day; he studied maps in the privacy of his office; and his continued insistence that he be provided with new shallow-draft gunboats convinced his staff that he was thinking in terms of a new campaign.

General Sherman visited Porter at Christmas time and they discussed the intricacies of that campaign. In short, Porter had decided to strike a major blow against the Confederacy west of the Mississippi. The Red River, 1,018 miles long, reaching into Texas and Arkansas, cut through rich agricultural country, and Porter wanted not only to cut off this breadbasket but to render the Red unsafe for Confederate naval raiders. He intended to take the city of Shreveport, located in northwestern Louisiana, at the head of the Red's navigable waters. If he succeeded, he would not only cause Louisiana to surrender to the Union, but would make it far more difficult for isolated Texas to remain in the Confederacy.

His chief problem was one of personnel. Since New Orleans was now included in his command, he was obliged to work with Major General Banks, whom he disliked. He wanted Sherman to march with him, but the general had his sights set on taking Atlanta. Sherman, who also had little faith in Banks, finally agreed to release one of his divisions — a unit of ten thousand men — to participate in the campaign.

The gunboats, steamers, and rams gathered at captured Vicksburg, and early in March, 1864, Porter sailed down the Mississippi from Cairo to join his command. The new expedition was under way. Banks, with twenty thousand men, was scheduled to meet the Navy at Alexandria, on the Red River, and another ten thousand were ordered to march through the Arkansas River country from Little Rock and rendezvous with Banks near Shreveport.

History repeated itself in the opening days of the campaign. Fort de Russy had been rebuilt by the Confederates, but Porter's ironclads smashed through the river barriers, and the defenders fled. Sherman's division — the first Army troops to reach the scene — were disappointed when they discovered the enemy had disappeared. A light-draft force was sent up the river, but the Confederates made good their escape.

While waiting for Banks, who did not bring his columns into Alexandria until March 25th and 26th, more than a week behind schedule, Porter kept his men busy collecting cotton and foodstuffs from the plantations of the area. When Banks arrived, he did nothing to inspire confidence. Although he knew that Sherman's division could remain with him for only a month, he dallied at Alexandria, where he established a major supply base requiring the services of four thousand of his men. After quarreling with the commander of a Marine brigade on loan to him, he sent the brigade back to its base at Vicksburg, thus depriving his command of another three thousand men. Only when Porter threatened to proceed without him did he consent to move.

On March 31st, the Mississippi Squadron's shallow-draft ships started up the winding Red River, and the Army troops began their overland march. By April 10th, Porter's flotilla reached Springfield Landing, forty miles below Shreveport, where a courier from Banks was expected to be waiting for the admiral. The messenger was not there, and the ships pushed another ten miles upstream. There, the delayed courier finally reached the squadron, and Porter heard news he could scarcely believe. Banks had suffered a major defeat and his troops were in full flight.

Without military land support, the squadron was compelled to turn back. But the voyage downstream was grim from the outset. The water level fell, making it necessary to tow the transports carrying food and ammunition. Confederate Brigadier General Thomas Green and his six thousand men, having disposed of Banks, were now free to attack the Union Navy force from the heights in the hilly river country. Porter, undaunted as ever, proved himself equal to this new situation. When Confederate cavalry made their expected appearance, the cannon emplaced on his ironclads took a heavy toll of horses and men, completely scattering the enemy.

On April 15th, Porter and Banks finally met at the little Red River village of Grand Ecore. Banks insisted on continuing his retreat, using the return of Sherman's division to its parent command as his reason. Porter realized that without Army support he could not remain on the Red River, and was worried about the ten thousand men already marching through the wilderness from Little Rock toward Shreveport. Immediately he sent off a letter to Sherman, explaining the situation and asking for the continued use of the division until he attained his objective. The thought of turning back never occurred to him. He prepared for the worst, returning his heavier draft ships to the Mississippi, and giving orders to his subordinate commanders, to send him their shallow-draft gunboats.

Meanwhile, General Banks having ordered his troops to retreat to Alexandria, he had to fend off Confederate guerrillas alone. The flotilla had no choice now, and was forced to pull back to Alexandria. Porter fought grimly and doggedly all the way, his ships conspicuous targets for Confederates who could hide in the woods beyond sight of the Navy gunners.

The battered Union vessels reached Alexandria in late April, and the river continued to fall so drastically that Porter was afraid his ships would be marooned above the Alexandria Rapids. Banks again swore he would not abandon the squadron, but a bitter Porter was no longer able to believe anything the general told him. And the situation was rendered even more precarious by the receipt of a letter from Ulysses Grant — who had just been promoted to lieutenant general, and was unaware of what was taking place in Louisiana — directing Sherman's division to return at once to its parent command.

Lieutenant Colonel Joseph Bailey of the 4th Wisconsin Cavalry saved the squadron from disaster when he suggested that the falls be dammed and the ships floated over them.

Porter agreed, and thousands of men were put to work cutting down trees. This operation began on April 30th, and on May 8th the upper falls were dammed. All of the ships were carried to safety. Only one gunboat scraped the bottom badly enough to slash a hole in her bottom and this was quickly repaired. The second dam was easier to construct, and was completed by the afternoon of May 11th. By noon on May 12th, the ships had been floated to deeper waters, and were able to sail on to the mouth of the Red River without further incident.

Having gone without sleep for weeks, Porter collapsed when Fleet Captain Breese met him, and had to be carried on board his flagship, the *Black Hawk*. A physician was summoned, and diagnosed the illness as a return of his fever. Only a man of indomitable will could have worked around the clock as Porter had done, with his body racked by fever.

His real sickness, however, was one of the spirit. It did not matter to him that he had conducted himself honorably and commanded his force ably. For the first time in his life he had suffered total failure, and his despair was far more debilitating than the fever.

While the *Black Hawk* carried him back up the river to Cairo, the Confederate newspapers at last had a reason to rejoice. Admiral Porter, the "conqueror of the Mississippi," had been defeated by Confederate guerrillas and had been sent running, his proud gunboats badly battered.

Newspapers in the North also made a great furor over the retreat, and Porter's name went under a cloud. But gradually the truth about the campaign began to emerge, and General Banks was given most of the blame. The Navy Department firmly upheld its admiral, and both Secretary Welles and Assistant Secretary Fox were insistent in pointing out that the ultimate culprit was the War Department. If Shreveport had been worth taking, they said, Sherman's division or some comparable unit should have been assigned to the Army command in the West on a permanent basis.

Generals Grant and Sherman both wrote long, sympathetic letters to Porter. As soon as his health permitted, he replied in the same vein. It is significant that his friendship with the two most prominent Union commanders survived the fiasco.

Porter displayed remarkable recuperative powers, and when the *Black Hawk* reached Cairo, after a week's voyage, he avidly read the latest war news. General Grant had taken command of the Union Army in Virginia, and was contesting the Confederate commander in chief, General Robert E. Lee. Meanwhile, Sherman, marching on Atlanta, was putting into effect what later would become known as a "scorched earth" policy, destroying food supplies, railroads, and public buildings — in short, anything and everything that enabled the South to wage war.

It was Porter's opinion that the Navy should concentrate on a strategic goal similar to Sherman's and try to isolate the Confederacy completely from the outside world. He saw the specific mission of the Mississippi Squadron as one of choking off the smuggling operations that helped the Confederates obtain provisions, armaments, and cloth. His first self-appointed task, when he sat down at his desk in Cairo, was that of reorganizing his command and ordering his principal subordinates to halt all smuggling.

His theater of operations, he realized, would be of minor importance in the future. But he did not think it possible, after the failure of the Red River campaign, that he would be given the opportunity to play a more active role in the war. In fact, there was a good chance that if Grant and Sherman were successful in their respective campaigns, it might bring total victory for the Union.

Turning to his personal mail, Porter learned from a letter from his mother that his brother, William, had died on May 1st in a New York hospital before his court-martial trial could be held. So, regrettably but unavoidably, another permanent stain tarnished the Porter name. Georgy wrote more cheerfully that she was planning to spend the summer with friends in New Jersey and would take the younger children with her.

Early in June he received a letter from the Assistant Secretary of the Navy, in which Fox congratulated him for his feat in extricating his squadron from a seemingly hopeless predicament on the Red River. A casual final sentence read: "After you get your feathers smoothed and oiled, I don't see why you should not come East, if you so desire it."

Two days later another unofficial letter reached Cairo, this one from Secretary Welles, who wrote, "You may want to arrange your command so you can absent yourself from it for a short period. If so, I would be pleased to see you in Washington."

It was almost too much for Porter to hope that he would be given a new and challenging assignment.

XI

ADMIRAL DAVID PORTER reached Washington on July 6, 1864, and after friendly talks with his civilian superiors, was granted a leave of absence. Joining his family at Perth Amboy, New Jersey, he spent his days frolicking with his younger children — and exchanging daily telegrams with Captains Breese and Pennock. Even though he was enjoying a holiday, he continued to command his squadron from a distance.

Early in August, Admiral Farragut's fleet successfully sealed off Mobile, the last important Confederate port on the Gulf of Mexico, and General Sherman took Atlanta. The war had entered its final, decisive phase, and Porter was summoned to Washington.

After many conferences, it was decided to give him command of a squadron with a specific mission — that of destroying the Confederate naval base at Wilmington, North Carolina, an important headquarters for sea raiders that were still sinking vast numbers of Union commercial ships. General Grant agreed to supply a coordinating military force.

Reluctant to take a command involving cooperation with the Army, Porter nevertheless obeyed orders and tried to forget the Red River disaster. He made a trip to Cairo for the purpose of putting his command there in shape for his successor, and then traveled to Hampton Roads, Virginia, taking his family with him.

His new command, he learned, would be comprised of eighty-seven ships, some ironclads and some wooden sailing ships. Under him were five commodores, all senior to him in service, but none displayed any jealousy over his rapid rise in rank. Captain Breese became his fleet captain, and he hired his son, Carlisle, as his flag secretary.

While the ships were being repaired, painted, and provisioned, with new crews assigned to them, he paid a visit to General Grant in the field, and felt uneasy when he discovered that the Army commander was less than enthusiastic about the campaign. That feeling became more intense when Major General Benjamin Butler, with whom Porter had clashed at New Orleans, was assigned the command of the Army task force. For the sake of harmony, he took Georgy with him and paid a call on Mrs. Butler in Norfolk.

The troops had been promised by October 15th, but did not appear on time. Irked by the delay, he sent some of his ships to blockade Wilmington. "When in doubt," his order said, "attack!" The directive soon became famous, and quickly produced results. Within two weeks almost three million dollars worth of Confederate prize vessels and cargoes fell into the hands of the North Atlantic Blockading Squadron, as the fleet was called.

Anxious to take both Wilmington and the principal Confederate bastion on the North Carolina coast, Fort Fisher, Porter complained repeatedly, but in vain, to the Navy when Butler continued his dilatory tactics. Welles and Fox were unable to prod Butler, so David made a direct appeal to Grant. The general-in-chief was in command of all Union troops, but he, too, was powerless to force Butler to act.

Early in December — when the Confederates transferred several units from Wilmington to reinforce their garrison at Savannah, which Sherman was attacking — seemed to be an auspicious time to make a move. Grant paid a visit to Hampton Roads and dined with Porter on board his flag ship, the *Malvern*. During the course of their meeting the general vowed that the troops would march against Wilmington within seventy-two hours.

Unfortunately, a winter storm made it impossible for the bulk of Porter's squadron to move into the open sea until December 8th. By that time Butler was nowhere to be found. Recalling the situation that had prevailed at New Orleans, Porter registered new, official complaints. Butler learned of his reports, and relations between the two men became increasingly strained.

On December 16th, after the squadron had put to sea, intending to make the attack alone should it prove to be necessary, Butler appeared with his troops on board transports. The attack on Fort Fisher finally began with a Navy bombardment on December 23rd. For forty-eight hours the ships' cannon pounded the Confederates, who replied with their own heavy fire.

On Christmas Day the Army landings began. Approximately three thousand of Butler's men — less than half of his total command — went ashore while the general, on board his transport, watched the operation through his glasses. According to the joint operational plan, the Army was supposed to storm Fort Fisher, but Butler learned through a prisoner that a full division of Confederate troops had just arrived from Richmond to bolster Fort Fisher's defenses. Rather than risk an engagement with a superior force, Butler ordered a withdrawal. Not bothering to wait for it to be accomplished, he sailed away.

Porter was furious, in part because Butler had not consulted him before directing his troops to break off contact with the enemy, and partly because he had removed himself from the scene without waiting for the squadron to evacuate his troops.

Lieutenant S. W. Preston, Porter's aide-de-camp, subsequently revealed that the admiral completely lost his temper when he saw Butler's transport departing. At one point he contemplated using force to compel the vessel to turn back, but was dissuaded by Captain Breese and other members of the staff.

Newspaper correspondents who had accompanied the squadron were unanimous in their opinions about the handling of the action. *The New York Times* declared that Admiral Porter's men had fought diligently and courageously, but that the Army units had been given no opportunity to show their worth.

Porter was so disgusted that he sent Lieutenant Preston to Washington the following day. Preston carried a written plea for an Army task force under a different commander, and to it he added Porter's urgent verbal request. Captain Breese was sent to the Union Army's headquarters outside Savannah to ask General Sherman if he would participate in the attack on Wilmington. Although sympathetic, Sherman had other work to do, and wrote Porter a long letter of commiseration.

Positive that Fort Fisher could be taken, Porter sent another desperate message to Secretary Welles. But the War Department had no additional men to spare, even though Fort Fisher had been reinforced by the Confederates, and Welles replied that the best promise he had been able to obtain from the War Department was that a new general would be assigned to command the same six thousand, five hundred men who had comprised the original task force.

Success had become imperative, even though the odds against it had become higher. Porter well knew that, even though Army commanders had twice been directly responsible for his inability to complete missions, another failure would ruin his reputation. No matter how blameless his own conduct had been, the Government and the public at large would claim he had been promoted too rapidly, and would demand his retirement from active duty.

For the present, he was in the clear. Not only had his civilian supporters in the Navy given him their unquestioning support, but President Lincoln, after making a study of what had happened at Fort Fisher, ordered General Butler to be relieved of command and sent home pending an investigation, thus putting the blame on the Army officer-politician. However, Porter was worried because Butler had friends in Congress and among influential newspaper publishers. If another attack should fail, Ben Butler's cohorts would insist that Butler had been made a scapegoat.

For the sake of his own future as well as that of attaining his assigned objective, Porter realized he had to keep risks to a minimum. He made his plans almost literally overnight — and they were brilliant. On January 1, 1865, he began to withdraw his squadron from Wilmington and Fort Fisher. Deliberately hoping to convince the Confederates that he had been knocked out of action, he withdrew his ships two and three at a time. Pretending that most of them — steam vessels and sailing ships alike — were disabled, he had them towed until they could no longer be seen by watchers on the coast.

The ruse succeeded. The Richmond *Whig,* claiming a victory, asked in a jubilant editorial, "Where is the intrepid Porter now? His 'invincible' fleet has been beaten, scattered, sunk, dispersed all over the Atlantic Ocean!"

The squadron quietly returned to Hampton Roads and took on fresh supplies of water and food, as well as stores of ammunition and gunpowder. A secret conference of all captains was held in the admiral's quarters on the *Malvern* during which Porter revealed the next step to them. Every able-bodied seaman who could be spared was to be enrolled in a special landing force; in other words, the sailors would act as soldiers. A total of one thousand, six hundred men were assigned to the force, and to them he added the four hundred Marines of his squadron. Like all Marines, the latter were elite troops, capable of handling any situation. These two thousand, the admiral said, would be the first ashore, and would secure and hold the beach for the Army regiments that would follow them.

Porter could not have known that he had invented a new technique of warfare, and that, in the next century, combined amphibious Marine-Navy-and-Army forces would make landing after landing in World War II.

On January 6th, Major General A. H. Terry was given command of the Army forces previously under Butler. An alert, aggressive officer, Terry immediately conferred with Porter, concurred in his plans, and promised that the Army would redeem itself. That same day he paraded his troops, then made a speech calculated to instill new pride in them. Without revealing the object of the forthcoming offensive, he told them they would be given, in the immediate future, a great opportunity to redeem themselves and the good names of their regiments.

Gales prevented the start of the expedition for several days, and Porter was later described by correspondents for the *New York Herald* and *Chicago Tribune* as a "caged lion," both using the same phrase. He paced the decks of the *Malvern*, indifferent to the elements, and demanded hourly weather reports, intending to get under way as soon as he heard that the skies were beginning to clear.

The weather began to improve in mid-afternoon on January 11th. The seas were still heavy, but at dusk, when movements could not be seen by any patrolling Confederate agents, the squadron slipped out into the white-capped waters, escorting General Terry's transports. What was destined to be Admiral David Porter's last major operation in the Civil War had begun.

At dawn on January 13th the relaxed defenders of Fort Fisher were awakened by the rumble of a furious bombardment. Sentinels on the artillery ramparts, peering off into the early morning haze, reported that Porter's ships had returned. The ironclads maintained a steady fire, gunners working at the rapid pace their commander demanded. The smaller gunboats, ignoring the heavy swell that increased the danger of their being swept onto the rocks adjacent to the fort, edged close to land and poured shells into the double lines of palisades.

The startled Confederates replied as fast as their gunners could race to their battle stations, but they had already lost the initiative. And the Union seamen demonstrated a seemingly reckless indifference to the fate of their ships, not to mention their lives. Paying no attention to the shot hurled at them by the shore batteries, the ironclads held their positions and threw broadside after broadside at the fort. So rapidly were the Union cannon fired, reloaded, and fired again that many of the men in the fort believed the strength of the attacking squadron had been doubled.

At Porter's suggestion, General Terry had sailed with him on the *Malvern*, and the two senior officers of the expedition stood together on the ironclad's upper deck, observing the effect of the deadly bombardment. At 8:45 A.M. they agreed that the time had come to go ashore. Within a quarter of an hour the Navy's boats were lowered into the choppy water. The first to wade through the surf and climb over rocks onto the picnic grounds beyond the fort were the Marines.

By three o'clock that afternoon a total of eight thousand men had gone ashore. Trenches were dug; small mortars were emplaced for purposes of defense; and, the landing having been secured, the Marines and sailors returned to their ships. General Terry, who had been a member of the initial landing party, established sentry outposts, and the Army task force, guarded by the Navy's ironclads, settled down for an uneasy night.

Before dawn on January 14th, a gale blew in, making operations on either side impossible. The troops shivered in the trenches; the ironclads continued to cover the fort; and Porter ordered some of his wooden-hulled sailing ships out to sea, where they could ride out the storm without danger of being smashed on the rocks.

Late that night the storm subsided, and the ships moved into battle formation, again before daybreak. At dawn the bombardment of Fort Fisher was resumed, its tempo even more furious than that of the previous shelling. At 10:30 the admiral gave the signal, "Boarders away," and the landing boats filled with Marines and sailors started toward shore, this time toward a position close to the battered palisades.

Fleet Captain Breese, at his own insistence, led the invaders. Carlisle Porter, armed with a cutlass and pistol, took his place beside him, determined to prove his worth, even though he had been discharged from the Naval Academy. The admiral's flag was carried by his aides, both of whom were killed within the hour.

At a signal from General Terry, the Marines and sailors rushed toward the fort from the east, while the Army regiments climbed out of their trenches and simultaneously attacked from the west. The Marines had been assigned the task of picking off enemy sharpshooters on the palisades, and performed with admirable efficiency, even though their own casualty rate was high.

Meanwhile, the ironclads continued to pour heavy cannon fire into the fort. This was delicate work, with friendly forces on either side of the palisade-encircled stone buildings, and the gunners had been cautioned to exercise great care in placing their shots.

Late in the afternoon Porter, watching the engagement through his glasses from the *Malvern*'s upper deck, sent a message to Terry by semaphore: "Are we firing too close for the comfort of your men?"

"You are accurate," the general replied. "Keep firing."

Porter then asked Breese the same question.

The fleet captain had not lost his sense of humor. "You have at least two hundred feet to spare," he replied. "Continue fire unless notified otherwise."

Night came, but the darkness was punctuated by the flash of cannon fire from the ships and the fort, as well as the constant sputter of musket and pistol fire in what was becoming increasingly close combat.

At 9:00 P.M. Captain Breese sent up flares, signalling the admiral — "Cease fire." At that moment the Marines were climbing over the palisades and engaging in hand-to-hand combat with the grim defenders.

The warships fell silent. Reduced now to the role of a mere spectator, Porter paced up and down the *Malvern*'s decks, peering toward land and muttering that he wanted to take part in the climactic phase of the battle. According to the subsequent dispatches of newspaper correspondents on board the flagship, his staff members managed to dissuade him. But he was in a foul mood, and for a half hour no subordinate dared go near him.

Suddenly, at 10:00 P.M., General Terry sent up successive red, white, and blue flares, which meant that Fort Fisher had fallen.

All the ships of the squadron erupted in a spontaneous demonstration. Flares lighted the sky, and whistles screamed for hours. Meanwhile, the Marines, sailors, and soldiers were engaged in grim work. Dead and wounded were piled high in the many passages of the fort. Dawn had come before the wounded could be recovered and given superficial treatment. Later, when it was possible to move them, they were sent out to the hospital ship that had slid in close to shore.

A final tragedy took place less than an hour after sunrise. Several soldiers discovered the main powder magazine in the deep recesses of the fort, and went in to investigate its contents. Too late, officers tried to get them out. A sudden explosion rocked the entire fort, and two hundred Union troops were killed, most of them buried in the debris.

Porter immediately went ashore in his gig, using the route General Terry had taken, and examined the damage with Terry and Captain Breese. The better part of the fort's upper works had been demolished. Later in the morning, after the wounded men had been removed, the admiral went on an inspection tour of the entire defense perimeter, and said that he had never seen such magnificent works. Terry told him that his accurate gunnery had made it possible for the assault forces to take the place.

Wilmington was now sealed off, and the squadron's shallow-draft vessels moved up the Cape Fear River to prevent the city's defenders from escaping by sea. Meanwhile, Terry's regiments moved into position opposite the city, stringing out on the edge of rice fields that winter snow and rain had transformed into marshes. It was apparent that too few troops were on hand to accomplish the task of reducing Wilmington. Therefore, Porter elected to obtain reinforcements unofficially rather than go through the time-consuming process of making a request through the Navy Department, which would communicate with the War Department, which would then send the request to General Grant. It was far easier and more sensible to write Grant a personal letter — which he did.

The general took time out from his own campaign against Lee to pay Porter a visit. The two friends inspected Fort Fisher together, and made a tour of the Union lines outside Wilmington. Grant agreed that Terry needed reinforcements, and a fresh column was dispatched the following day, after he returned to his own headquarters.

Even with help, the investment of the city was a long, dreary process. Neither Porter nor Terry wanted to harm civilians, so no general shelling of Wilmington was permitted. Instead, the troops edged closer and closer to the entrenchments the Confederates had thrown up around the city, while Navy vessels inched up the river, demolition experts removing charges placed there in the hope the ships of the approaching squadron would be destroyed.

The end at Wilmington was anticlimactic. In the early hours of the morning, on February 22nd, the remnant of the Confederate garrison withdrew, abandoning the city. The attackers learned of their disappearance when civilians approached them, carrying white flags. Wilmington was occupied before breakfast, and General Sherman thereby gained an important base for his operations against the Confederate corps defending the approaches to Richmond from the south.

Porter returned to sea, and his squadron stood off the coast of Virginia to intercept ships bringing supplies from Europe to Lee's hard-pressed forces. It was obvious to everyone, including the entire squadron, that the war was drawing to a close, and many of the sailors, whose enlistment would last only until peace came, were growing restless. Because he realized that a disciplinary problem might arise, Porter sent a message to all his commodores and captains:

"General Grant's men are still dying each day. Contrary to rumors heard throughout this fleet, the enemy has not yet surrendered. Until he does, we are still at war. Any defection from duty will be treated with the gravity it deserves. Captains are directed not to be sparing in calling boards to hear cases of dereliction of duty, and to treat such derelictions as they deserve in time of war. Captains are further directed to assemble their crews and to read this order to them."

At the beginning of March, the Congressional Joint Committee on the Conduct of the War summoned Porter to a hearing. Turning the squadron over to his senior commodore, he left at once for Washington, arriving on March 5th, the day after President Lincoln's second inauguration.

On March 7th he appeared before the committee, spending the morning telling them what had happened on the Red River expedition and the first campaign against Fort Fisher. In the afternoon the members of the committee questioned him on both matters. In true Porter fashion, he did not express himself diplomatically. He freely told the committee what he thought of both General Banks and General Butler, and offended several of Butler's friends. But he refused to spare anyone, and was indifferent to the committee's reaction. "They didn't get at the truth," he said at a later date, "nor did they desire to do so."

Secretary Welles rewarded the successful admiral by transferring him to the command of the City Squadron, with headquarters in Washington. This enabled Porter to live at home for the first time in years, and since his duties were light, he had an opportunity to relax. In the following weeks he spent a great deal of time with President Lincoln, escorting him on tours behind the Union lines and, occasionally, riding with him across the fields for an hour's exercise.

General Grant was making his headquarters at City Point, Virginia, and Porter accompanied the President there when Lincoln paid a farewell visit to Generals Grant and Sherman before the final campaign of the war was undertaken.

Lincoln seemed to enjoy Porter's company, and one anecdote of the time they spent together has endured: "I don't think," Lincoln said one day, referring to Ben Butler, "that your friend, the general, was very much of an engineer."

"I agree with you, Mr. President," Porter said.

Lincoln was lost in thought for a moment. "It crosses my mind," he said, "that your friend, the general, wasn't much of a general, either."

Porter, doubling up with laughter, agreed again.

The entire North rejoiced when General Lee surrendered to General Grant at Appomattox Court House on April 9th, and the following day Porter went out to sea on the U.S.S. *Tristram Shandy*, a small steamer. It was typical of him that, in this hour of relief from the pain that the war had brought to all Americans, he wanted to be alone — and at sea.

On April 15th he put into Baltimore, and was shocked to hear of President Lincoln's assassination the previous night. He went at once to Washington, by train, and hurried to the Navy Department, where he learned that the news was true.

Abraham Lincoln was dead. Openly and without shame, Porter wept, unmindful of the presence of junior officers and clerks.

"The United States," he wrote to his mother, "has lost the greatest man she has ever produced."

An era truly had come to an end, and David Dixon Porter realized that he had come out of the war a vastly changed man. In a little more than three years he had moved rapidly from the rank of lieutenant to that of rear admiral. Not only had his naval exploits made history, but he had emerged from the conflict as a figure of consequence, a leader who had demonstrated his worth to his country, a strategist and tactician who had won the respect of colleagues throughout the world. He knew, too, that his career was far from ended, that he still had major contributions to make.

XII

THE United States followed her historical traditions at the end of the Civil War, and there was a general demobilization in the armed services. The Navy sent thousands of volunteer officers and seamen back to civilian life, and many career officers, no longer needed, were retired. Hundreds of warships were decommissioned, and scores of naval installations were closed.

Rear Admiral David Porter correctly assumed that he would remain on active duty. Secretary of the Navy Welles and Assistant Secretary Fox, both of whom remained in office after President Andrew Johnson succeeded Abraham Lincoln, were keenly aware of his worth and intended to utilize his talents. The only problem they faced was that of determining how to employ him.

Displaying typical vigor, Porter settled the question himself. Still deeply interested in the Naval Academy, he obtained a leave of absence and made an extended trip to Newport, Rhode Island, the wartime home of the academy. On his way back to Washington he stopped for several days at Annapolis, Maryland, the school's permanent site. Everything he learned confirmed his uneasy suspicions. The academy, founded in the middle of the century during the administration of President James K. Polk, was out of tune with the times.

Its training program was woefully inadequate. The war had proved for all time that sailing vessels were outmoded and that henceforth navies would be comprised of steam-propelled ironclads, but midshipmen were still being taught to operate wooden-hulled ships driven by sails. The academic curriculum was made up of courses mainly in Latin, the classics, and mathematics. David was chagrined to discover that the academy's library, which had been shipped to Newport, had remained untouched throughout the war. The books had not been removed from their packing cases.

Worst of all, he discovered that no intensive efforts were being made to train the midshipmen as officers, teach them the Navy's traditions, or give them a feeling of pride in the service. The atmosphere was not only hopelessly conservative, but was so Puritanical that, as he later told Assistant Secretary Fox, "A graduate of the school is better suited for a life in the pulpit than a life at sea."

After his return to Washington, Porter held several long talks with the secretary and assistant secretary, and early in the summer of 1865 was given the appointment he wanted, that of Superintendent of the Naval Academy.

In September of that year, after the superintendent's house had been cleaned and redecorated, the Porter family moved in. At one time or another during the first year of their occupancy, all six of the children lived there. David Essex, who at twenty had held the rank of brevet (temporary) captain in the infantry, was at home with his parents until he obtained a commission in the Regular Army as a first lieutenant. Carlisle continued to work as his father's flag secretary, but had no desire to remain a civilian. Refusing to allow influence to be used on his behalf, he eventually won a commission in the Marine Corps, where he enjoyed a fruitful career.

Theodoric, who was sixteen, entered the academy as a midshipman in the autumn of 1865, and swiftly learned that he enjoyed no special status because he was the admiral's son. By the time he won his commission, his classmates said that he had stood more hours of sentry duty than any other cadet. Theodoric was an excellent fencer, ranking first in the sport at the academy, and also did well in French, Latin, and Greek. Mathematics almost proved to be his undoing, but a summons to the admiral's office and a subsequent long, difficult session behind closed doors spurred him on to improvement.

Richard, who was eleven in 1865, was blunt, honest to a fault, and independent — in short, a typical Porter. He was sent to the Chester Military School, but hated what he termed a regimented life, and eventually made a highly successful career for himself in business.

The two girls — Elizabeth, who was 13 in 1865, and Elena, who was 9 — attended a nearby school, rode every afternoon with their father, and helped their mother entertain. Almost inevitably, Elizabeth fell in love several years later with a cadet. Her parents recognized Midshipman Leavitt C. Logan's unusual qualities, and eventually, after he rose to the rank of lieutenant, he and Elizabeth were married.

Meanwhile, one of the first steps taken by Porter after his appointment was to obtain the services of Captain K. R. Breese, his closest associate in the war, as assistant superintendent. Together they combed the lists of officers on active duty to obtain the best possible faculty. At the same time, Porter requested funds for the new buildings and equipment he believed vital for training young men as officers in a modern navy.

Congress balked, not wanting to give the armed forces more money than was essential in peacetime. Porter appeared before committees of both Houses of Congress, and was so vigorous in expressing his convictions that he was voted all he needed.

New classroom buildings and barracks for the cadets were constructed, and, for the first time, athletic fields were laid out. Steam engines, propellers, turret monitors, and electric batteries were obtained for practical classroom study.

Laboratories for the study of astronomy and geographic survey were built, and he brought a number of mortars, rifled guns of various caliber, and tons of ammunition to the academy for field work utilization. He also acquired a small fleet of ships for the exclusive use of the cadets and their instructors, some to be used as classrooms, others for training cruises.

One was a fully equipped survey ship. There were two ironclads and a ram; and a smaller gunboat was hauled inside one of the new buildings for classroom use. Believing that the principles of navigation could best be learned on the old sailing ships, however, he also obtained a square-rigger for use on cruises. And a special laboratory was constructed to house torpedoes, which alarmed the residents of Annapolis, who were afraid that student experiments might blow up the town. Then, in a final triumphant move, Porter acquired the U.S.S. *Constitution* when he learned that no one else wanted "Old Ironsides."

Civilians were hired to make a large number of model engines, torpedoes, fuses, guns, and even ships. These were assigned to the heads of academic departments, each of whom was ordered to revise his own curriculum.

The departments of English, Mathematics, Astronomy, Classics, and Philosophy sought the help of professors at Harvard and Yale in laying out new courses of study. The chaplain was made head of the department of Ethics — an innovation. New departments of Gunnery, Seamanship, Naval Tactics, and Navigation were established. So was a department of Steam Enginery under Chief Engineer W. W. W. Wood, whom the cadets soon called "Wee Willie Wonderful."

Above all, Porter created a new spirit. Discipline was strict, but was administered, in the main, by upper-class midshipmen. An honor system was introduced, and the old tradition of tattling, or student spying, was strictly forbidden. A demerit system was installed, and cadets worked out their demerits by marching sentry duty, which they loathed. When it became necessary for the faculty to discipline a midshipman, he was tried by a board of inquiry. If found guilty, he was placed in solitary confinement on a diet of bread and water. The hazing of new cadets was prohibited. When the superintendent discovered that his injunction was being ignored, he instructed the staff to haze the upperclassmen. His order was carried out so effectively that hazing promptly halted.

The order establishing the academy in 1845 had provided that cadets be trained to be gentlemen as well as officers, but this stipulation had been ignored, in the main, by previous superintendents. Porter remembered his own tours of duty as a midshipman, and cadets were taught how to dance and behave in the company of ladies, use good table manners, and learn the principles of etiquette. In order to encourage the midshipmen in these practices, the superintendent and Mrs. Porter held monthly receptions at which the attendance of cadets was obligatory.

Good health was stressed, and cadets were given rigorous periodic physical examinations. Regular bathing was required, as were twice-monthly visits to the academy barbers. A compulsory gymnastics and marching program was introduced, and midshipmen were encouraged to engage in such extracurricular sports as fencing, boxing, riding, bowling, track, and sailing. Interclass meets were held regularly, and, to the delight of the cadets, Admiral Porter sometimes climbed into one of the rings installed in the new gymnasium for a bout with an upperclassman.

A dramatics club came into being, with feminine parts played by girls from nearby schools. An orchestra was formed, as was a glee club; the band was issued new uniforms of blue and gold, and, in a startling innovation, was led by a baton-wielding drum major. A debating society was organized, and on one memorable occasion the admiral matched himself against the varsity team, with a civilian board of judges diplomatically deciding that the contest was a draw.

The ascetic life that midshipmen had been forced to lead in the past was altered drastically. Houses were built on the academy grounds for faculty members who, for the first time, brought their wives and children to live with them. And young ladies were imported from Baltimore, Washington, and Philadelphia for special receptions.

Porter did not forget that he had been a practical joker as a midshipman, and, realizing he was dealing with boys, kept his sense of humor: "Midshipman Thompson, First Class, who plays so abominably on a fish horn," he wrote on one occasion, "will oblige me by going outside the limits when he wants to practice, or he will find himself coming out of the little end of the horn."

He tolerated no breaches of discipline, however, and when a class listening to a boring lecture in mechanics stomped their feet in unison, the offenders were required to stand sentry duty for ten consecutive hours in bitterly cold weather.

"I loosen or tighten the reins according as they conduct themselves," he wrote in a report to the Navy Department. "My rule is to bear with offending midshipmen as long as I think there is anything in them to justify keeping them here. Their insubordination can be checked with punishments, their mischiefs with guard duty." In a ringing declaration of principle he declared, "As long as a boy is only mischievous or full of life and spirit, I stand up for him."

In 1866, Vice Admiral Farragut, the first Navy officer ever to hold that high a rank, was unexpectedly given four stars and made a full admiral. Simultaneously his foster-brother, David Dixon Porter, was promoted to the three-star rank of vice admiral. Porter and Georgy celebrated by giving a dinner party for their good friends, including several Senators and Congressmen, a number of Navy officers and their wives, and two of Porter's wartime comrades, Ulysses S. Grant and William T. Sherman, both of whom brought their families to the party.

It was significant that the Porters, Grants, and Shermans saw a great deal of each other during the years David was stationed at the naval academy. All three officers were naturally conscious of their high rank, and Porter, who was close to Farragut, hoped and half-expected that he would some day assume the supreme command of the Navy, just as Sherman more or less anticipated that he would follow Grant as the Army commander. Apparently it did not occur to Porter that General Grant might become President. Like his father, Porter had no interest in politics, and politicians bored him.

He had learned, however, how to make an impression on civilians in high places when it suited his purposes. In the spring of 1867, he invited President Johnson to visit the naval academy, and for the better part of a week entertained Lincoln's successor with full-dress parades, a day's voyage on the *Constitution*, another on an ironclad to watch the midshipmen demonstrate their skill as gunners, and several dinner parties — some casual, and two elegantly formal.

There was a reason for Porter's hospitality. The naval academy had outgrown its site, thanks to the superintendent's energetic building program, and desperately needed room for further expansion. A mansion with extensive grounds adjoining the academy was owned by the state of Maryland, and formerly had been used as the governor's official dwelling. Although no official announcement had been made, Porter learned that the property was for sale, the state placing a price tag of three hundred thousand dollars on it.

Discreet inquiry had elicited the response that the Federal Government might be able to purchase the mansion and grounds for two hundred thousand dollars. But the President and Congress, immersed in the enormously expensive problems of Reconstruction, were in no mood to pay that sum for a further enlargement of the naval academy.

Porter handled the situation with skill and tact, and by the time Andrew Johnson returned to Washington he was an enthusiastic supporter of the vice admiral's program. In the following weeks, key Senators and Congressmen were entertained by Porter. Each was treated with care, according to the nature of his own personality. Some reviewed the regiment of cadets; others ate informal meals on the grounds of the superintendent's house; and still others made intensive inspections of classrooms, and interviewed the faculty.

The technique proved effective. In the autumn of 1867, a bill was quietly passed by Congress and signed by the President, authorizing the purchase of the desired property from the state of Maryland. Almost overnight there was ample space for all that Porter wanted to do. In fact, he was able to buy the property for only one hundred and fifty thousand dollars. He used the rest of the money to purchase three additional tracts, increasing the academy's property from twenty acres to almost one hundred and fifty.

Only Georgy knew that her husband suffered from ill health during his tour of duty as superintendent. Headaches sometimes blinded him, making it difficult for him to read, and the sweet foods he craved for the first time in his life gave him indigestion. He complained privately to his wife of what he called "neuralgia," and became so stiff when sitting at his desk that he designed a new, high desk, which Navy carpenters made for him. Thereafter, he wrote his reports, letters, and other documents while standing at it.

Georgy finally prevailed upon him to submit to examinations by the academy's physicians. Since he appeared to be in good health, had a ruddy complexion, and rode daily, he demurred. But she kept after him, and her will finally prevailed. The doctors could find no physical defects, and told him he was suffering from a delayed reaction to the intense strains of the war years. Porter disagreed and insisted that the damp climate of Annapolis was at the root of his ailments.

Georgy thought the physicians were right, and privately wrote to Porter's mother, saying that he had never been bothered by the climate of Washington, which was more humid than that of Annapolis.

Evalina Porter was growing increasingly feeble, but her wit was unimpaired. She replied to her daughter-in-law: "You might want to remind David that he thrives on a life at sea, where the damp is more intense than Annapolis'. You have my sympathies, dear Georgy. When a man becomes a vice admiral, his disposition grows crochety."

Apparently the diagnosis of the physicians was correct. In the late autumn of 1868, even though Porter continued to live in Annapolis, his physical complaints gradually vanished and he again enjoyed the robust health with which he had been blessed throughout the better part of his life.

The Republican Party's nomination of General Grant for the Presidency in the early summer of 1868 took David completely by surprise. He appears to have been the only member of

Grant's inner circle of friends who knew literally nothing of Grant's political ambitions, even though prominent political and business interests had been working openly in the general's behalf for months. It would seem that, on the social occasions when the admiral and the general got together, neither had engaged in political discussions.

In any event, Porter was elated. A custom that had originated in the first administration of President George Washington, during the infancy of the United States, strictly prohibited officers on active duty in the armed services from taking partisan political roles. But Porter, the lifelong iconoclastic son of an iconoclast, refused to let custom stand in the way of friendship. He not only sent the Republicans a letter, on naval academy stationery, offering to campaign for his old comrade, but voluntarily issued a public statement praising Grant as a teetotaler.

Anyone who knew Ulysses S. Grant — or knew anything about him, as thousands of former Union soldiers did — realized he was no advocate of temperance. In fact, it was often said that he could drink more liquor, with less effect on him, than could any other man in the country.

Certainly Porter had no false illusions about Grant's habits. He always served champagne when Grant came to Annapolis for dinner, and kept a bottle of whisky in a cupboard so he and the general could enjoy a nip together when they settled down for an evening of companionable conversation. So the lie was deliberate, and can only be excused on the dubious grounds of Porter's enthusiastic endorsement.

Fortunately for the admiral's own reputation, Grant's fondness for alcoholic beverages was not a substantial issue in the campaign. The press virtually ignored the silly statement, and the Democrats, although hard-pressed to halt a landslide, failed to challenge Porter. But soon afterwards he was inviting more trouble.

On three occasions during the campaign Grant came to Annapolis for a quiet dinner and an evening of relaxation with his friend. Each time Porter not only turned out the regiment of cadets in his honor but greeted him with a twenty-one-gun salute, which was reserved for heads of state. The Democrats protested, demanding that Porter be either reprimanded or retired. He not only ignored the tempest, but repeated the gesture.

In the election, on November 3rd, Grant defeated Horatio Seymour of New York, and within a few days Washington was buzzing with rumors. The President-elect, it was said, quite naturally placed great confidence in his Army and Navy colleagues, and therefore intended to appoint a general and an admiral, respectively, as Secretaries of the Army and Navy. Grant himself refused to comment, but unidentified sources close to him were quick to point out a precedent. Washington's first Secretary of War, they reminded the nation, had been Major General Henry Knox, his artillery commander in the Revolutionary War.

Admiral Farragut, sixty-seven years of age and content with his post as uniformed commander of the Navy, let it be known that he had no interest in an appointment. As it happened, Grant was not thinking of making him Secretary, but Farragut did not know it. The logical candidate was the friend whom the President-elect trusted, admired, and respected.

Porter heard rumors that he might be made Secretary of the Navy, but brushed them aside. Once again he was being naive, and it apparently did not cross his mind that, having spent his entire life in the service, he might be made civilian head of the Navy. The realization came three weeks after the election, when General Sherman wrote him that Grant was seriously contemplating giving him the appointment.

Porter was alarmed and dismayed. In his opinion it would be a demotion to become Mr. Porter after enjoying the title of vice admiral, and it did not matter to him in the least that he would become civilian head of the Navy. He met Sherman in Washington for dinner, prior to Christmas, and although no details of their conversation have ever become a matter of public record, he made it clear that he had no wish to become Secretary of the Navy.

Since Grant had not mentioned the matter to him directly, he felt it would be inappropriate for him to go to the President-elect with a refusal of a post that had not yet been offered. Sherman, however, a mutual friend and colleague, could be trusted to act as a discreet messenger.

When and how General Sherman communicated with President-elect Grant is not known, but on New Year's Day, 1869, Porter proposed a toast, with obvious relish, at a family gathering: "I would like to drink," he said, "to the happy prospect of wearing this uniform for the rest of my days."

But Ulysses Grant was a stubborn man, and had made up his mind. He passed the word through an intermediary — perhaps Sherman — that he wanted Porter as Secretary of the Navy.

Vice Admiral David Porter was equally stubborn, and chose the *Army and Navy Journal*, which he knew Grant read regularly, as the medium for his reply. The periodical published an unsigned article stating that Porter, like Farragut, had no interest whatever in a civilian appointment. The article hinted, rather delicately, that he would refuse the offer in the event it should be made.

The Democrats, joined by some Republicans, were opposed to the appointment of Army and Navy officers to high civilian posts, and several bills were being prepared by members of both Houses of Congress to exclude them from such positions. Grant, new to the political jungle, was advised by Senators who were trying to guide him that the appointment of Regular Army or Navy officers might consolidate the half-formed anti-military elements in both the Senate and the House. The President-elect, not wanting to antagonize Congress before he took office, compromised by appointing as Secretary of War a businessman who, as a volunteer officer, had been a member of his staff. Congress could not and did not object to having former Brigadier General John A. Rawlins of Illinois in the War Department.

Still wanting David Porter as Secretary of the Navy, Grant temporized. He took office on March 4, 1869, and all other members of his Cabinet were announced. As the days passed, the Navy post remained vacant. Porter, conscious of the President's friendship and good intentions, but equally aware that his own career as an officer was in jeopardy, was forced to be patient and wait.

XIII

ON the morning of March 9, 1869, while David Porter was eating breakfast with his wife, a messenger arrived from Washington with word that President Grant wanted to see the admiral without delay. Porter left at once, traveling on a special train the President had sent for him.

President Grant was waiting, and plunged into business as soon as his visitor arrived. He had wanted to appoint Porter as Secretary of the Navy, he said, but had deemed it wiser to avoid a squabble with Congress. Therefore, he had found what he hoped would be a perfect solution. He was naming Adolph E. Borie, of Philadelphia, as Secretary. A wealthy merchant, who had contributed generously to the Republican campaign fund, Borie had one major handicap: he knew literally nothing about the Navy. However, if David was willing, the President wanted him to become Borie's "special assistant." He would have no title, but, in effect, would control the department.

Porter considered the President's request an order, but made one observation that reflected his doubts. His usefulness would depend on how effectively he and Borie could work together. The President had anticipated just such a reaction, and suggested that the two men get acquainted. Borie had arrived in Washington the previous day, and an immediate meeting was arranged. The admiral and the Philadelphia merchant conferred at Borie's hotel, went to lunch together, and then returned to the White House.

Both were enthusiastic, and Grant announced Borie's appointment the same day. As it turned out, Porter formed a friendship that endured for the rest of his life. The new secretary was an able executive, quick to grasp new concepts, and, without deferring unduly to the admiral, appreciated his experience. In return, Porter realized that Borie was endowed with a first-rate mind, and respected his intellect. Together they formed a potent team.

Immediately relieved of his duties as superintendent of the naval academy, Porter nevertheless continued to live with his family in Annapolis, his previous complaints about the climate there forgotten. He gave no reason for electing to commute to Washington. Certainly the arrangement was inconvenient, and sometimes became a hardship. When he stayed late at his Navy Department office, as he did several evenings each week, he found it necessary to remain overnight in the city instead of going home to sleep. Probably he chose to make it appear that his assignment was temporary, and he may have been trying to indicate, both to the Navy and the outside world, that he was exerting little influence on the new secretary.

If that was his intention, he failed. No one was fooled, and the *Army and Navy Journal* always spoke of "the Borie-Porter administration," as did most newspapers. From the outset it was evident that Porter was functioning as a co-secretary, although only Borie's signature appeared on official documents. The secretary and the admiral occupied adjoining offices, and conferred frequently.

The Navy, which had been almost moribund during the immediate post-war years following demobilization, suddenly sprang to life. Clerks who had lazed away their working hours, loafing and chatting, were now frantically busy. Staff officers who had reported for duty late each morning and had gone home early every afternoon were as punctual as they would have been standing watches at sea. The New York *Herald* reported that in the first forty-eight hours after Borie and

Porter moved in, more general orders were issued than had been forthcoming in the previous two years.

Boards were formed to examine ships and engines, armaments, and technical equipment. Teams of officers and civilians were dispatched to inspect the Navy's yards and bases. Specialists studied the procurement of provisions and the condition of stores on hand. Other officer-civilian teams interviewed the Navy's uniformed personnel and civilian employees to ascertain their morale. Impartial experts were borrowed from the Treasury to comb through procurement accounts, payrolls, and other ledgers.

Since there had been so little to do in recent years, there had been a strong tendency at Navy headquarters — as in all other bureaucratic governmental organizations throughout history — to make the administrative processes more complex, thus giving idle officials some semblance of activity. Borie and Porter ruthlessly slashed red tape, simplified procedures, and, with the enthusiastic cooperation of Admiral Farragut, tried to instill in Navy offices the unity and crisp order that prevailed on board a ship.

One of the most vexing questions the newcomers faced was that of the "relative" rank of engineers, surgeons, paymasters, and other officers who performed so-called "service" duties and held staff positions rather than function in the direct chain-of-command of line officers. Until the Civil War had ended such officers were known only in connection with the work they performed, and were simply called "surgeon," "engineer," or whatever. Then Secretary Welles had ruled that these staff officers could rank with line officers after fewer years of service. As a line officer who had spent a lifetime in the Navy before achieving the rank of commander, Porter naturally sympathized with the line officers.

Trying to be fair to the service officers, however, he believed that each of them — the physicians and surgeons, the engineers — should have a separate corps, and be promoted within that corps according to standards laid down by a special board of admirals that would study the question and make its recommendations to the secretary. He also firmly believed, however, that line officers should take precedence, on all occasions, over service officers. Members of Congress friendly to him, and to Borie, drew up a bill incorporating these ideas; in effect, the measure provided for the reorganization of the Navy.

Gideon Welles, who had retired to his home in Hartford, Connecticut, when Grant had become President, watched the upheaval in the Navy with a jaundiced eye, and became convinced that his own efforts and policies were being repudiated. His friends, including members of Congress and such newspaper publishers as Horace Greeley of the New York *Tribune*, promptly counterattacked, accusing Borie and Porter of attempting to destroy the democratic base on which the Navy rested.

The uproar became so intense that President Grant, always sensitive to criticism, intervened in late May and ordered that the Borie-Porter efforts to readjust the relative rank of service officers be halted. In a gesture intended to demonstrate that his directive did not indicate a lack of faith in Porter or a change in their personal relationship, the President paid a visit to the Porters in Annapolis and was the guest of honor at a party that lasted until the small hours of the morning.

Secretary Borie, who was frustrated and annoyed by Washington politics, decided after spending only five weeks in office that he preferred the life he had known in Philadelphia to that of being a Cabinet officer. He resigned a few weeks later, and, in the interim, granted Porter full power to sign all documents and orders on behalf of the secretary. So, for all practical purposes, Vice Admiral Porter was Acting Secretary of the Navy. He remained in this unique position for a period of about four months.

Members of Congress who were opposed to the control of a major Government department by an officer on active duty criticized every move Porter made, as did many administration officials, some of whom were jealous of the authority he exercised. He continued to do his duty as he saw fit, however, and even after the appointment of George Robeson as Secretary of the Navy, his influence remained virtually undiminished. Those who disliked him bided their time.

On August 14, 1870, Admiral David Glasgow Farragut died at the Portsmouth, New Hampshire, Navy Yard while on an inspection tour. Everyone in the Navy believed that the only vice admiral would be given a fourth star, and the *Army and Navy Journal* said that the promotion of Admiral Porter was "a foregone conclusion." No one was surprised, therefore, when, in mid-September, President Grant signed Porter's new commission and sent his appointment to the Senate for what was expected to be an automatic confirmation.

But Congress was not in session, and the admiral's enemies mobilized against him for the purpose of blocking his appointment. Leading the attack was former Secretary Gideon Welles, who was still convinced that Porter was deliberately trying to reverse every policy he had established while in office. Welles fired the first salvo by writing a bitterly vindictive assault on the vice admiral in an influential magazine, *Galaxy*.

Welles had a powerful ally in General Benjamin Butler, who had returned to the House of Representatives. Together they concocted a high-explosive depth charge that, hopefully, would blast the four-star admiral-designate out of Washington and, perhaps, the Navy itself.

Immediately after Butler's miserable failure during the first attack on Fort Fisher at the end of 1864, Porter had written a blunt, angry letter of condemnation to Secretary Welles. In addition, he had let his temper becloud his judgment and had blamed General Grant for allowing Butler to hold a command for which he had been unsuited.

Welles remembered the letter, which he had placed in the Navy's files, and a clerk who was friendly to Butler removed it. On December 2, 1870, two New York newspapers, the *Sun* and the *World*, printed the document. President Grant, always sensitive to criticism from any source, was shocked by the seeming hypocrisy of someone he had long considered an intimate friend.

Porter was stunned. The letter, written in a careless moment, did not reflect his true feelings, and he realized he would have to act swiftly and decisively in order to convince the President that his friendship was genuine. First, he gave the New York *Herald* the private journal he had kept during the war, and the newspaper published excerpts which proved that he had always held Grant in high esteem. Then, on December 3rd, he wrote a long letter to the President, condemning himself for having made a hasty judgment, explaining that he had subsequently learned that Grant had not been responsible for Butler's appointment. The bulk of the letter was devoted to a forthright summation of the friendship they had enjoyed during the war and the years following it, when it had not occurred to either man that Grant might become President.

Instead of following the letter with a personal call on the President, as he had intended, Porter was sent to bed with an attack of pleurisy on December 4th. His illness was severe, and his physician insisted that he remain at home for almost three weeks. During this time the White House remained silent, and Porter suffered from intense depression, fearing he had lost a good friend.

When he returned to Washington on December 23rd, however, a White House military aide came to see him at his office, and told him that, should he care to go to the White House, the President would be pleased to receive him. He hurried to the Executive Mansion, and spent more than an hour closeted with Grant. Both men were smiling broadly when they emerged, their reconciliation complete.

The following day, newspapers throughout the country published the text of Porter's letter of apology to the President. It was hailed everywhere as an honorable expression of sentiment by a courageous man. Public opinion appeared to be swinging strongly in Porter's favor, and the President took pains, at his annual New Year's Day reception, to demonstrate his feeling of close kinship with the admiral.

Ben Butler was not discouraged, however, and launched violent daily assaults on the admiral from the sanctuary of the House floor. In speech after speech he insinuated that he possessed letters Porter had written that insulted Farragut, Sherman, and other military leaders. Porter was urged by his friends to ignore these attacks, but was temperamentally incapable of remaining silent. He challenged Butler to produce the letters.

The documents were not forthcoming, of course, since they were non-existent. But this did not deter Butler from maintaining his scurrilous barrage. The less responsible newspapers, interested only in sensationalism, printed his speeches.

On January 13, 1871, at 1:00 P.M., the Senate retired behind closed doors to debate the future of Vice Admiral Porter. Newspaper correspondents protested their exclusion in vain. Three hours later the doors were opened, and it was announced that Porter's promotion to the rank of full admiral had been confirmed by an overwhelming vote of thirty-one to ten. The first to congratulate him was his Army counterpart, General Sherman, who had been promoted to four-star rank in 1869, when he had succeeded Grant. Both officers went to the White House, and celebrated privately with the President.

A new life began for Porter and Georgy. As it was essential that they live in Washington, they bought a brick-and-stone mansion on H Street, in the heart of the city. A large, handsome house of three stories, it had been built a half-century earlier, and during the Civil War had been the official residence of the British Ambassador. Indicative of his rise in the world, Porter paid almost one hundred thousand dollars for the place, using a portion of his Civil War prize money for the purpose.

He could walk to his office in only five minutes, and reach the White House in even less time. Also, the property adjoined the Metropolitan Club, to which both he and Sherman belonged. Not only was the location perfect, but the horses he rode for exercise were kept in a spacious stable at the rear of the house.

Servants were needed to take care of the large establishment, and Porter installed an extensive wine cellar. Within the next two years he also purchased two summer homes, one at Narragansett, Rhode Island, the other at Perth Amboy, New Jersey. Since his salary was a relatively modest $13,000 a year, his scale of living caused comment in Washington. As it happened, he continued to receive considerable sums of Civil

War prize money throughout the 1870's, but not everyone knew this, and he was fated to suffer acute embarrassment.

Congress, increasingly economy-minded, cut down the Navy's appropriations each year, in spite of all that Porter did to encourage the maintenance of a large and powerful fleet. Necessity forced him to use other means.

He used his common sense and mechanical aptitudes to become an inventor, and his correspondence of the period indicates that desperation rather than a genuine inventor's urge inspired him. His first design, which was mass-produced, was a steel bowsprit that could be attached to an ordinary steamer in an hour's time — converting it into a ram — and could be removed as quickly. He also invented a new type of torpedo boat, and when tests proved his ideas feasible, improved on the original model. Before the decade ended he had invented a torpedo boat equipped with devices operated by electricity.

The U.S.S. *Alarm*, the first of these boats, proved so efficient and cost so little to build that the Navy subsequently was equipped with a whole fleet of such craft. It was estimated that Porter had saved the Navy more than ten million dollars while keeping the fleet at maximum strength.

Only a few months after Porter's promotion his aged mother died, and his grief was somewhat assuaged by the knowledge that she had seen him rise to the highest rank attainable in his profession. He buried her beside his father in a Philadelphia cemetery.

Three of the Porter sons and their daughter, Elizabeth, were married in the early 1870's, and within a few years the house on H Street was filled with visiting grandchildren. The bearded admiral, who terrified subordinates, awed Congressmen, and impressed distinguished European visitors, was transformed by his children's children. He romped with them and their friends, inventing endless new games for their entertainment — and his own. One afternoon, in 1877, several startled newspaper correspondents saw him skipping down the street, in full uniform, while two of his granddaughters, clutching his hands and shrieking with delight, followed his example. The stern disciplinarian who had reared his own sons and daughters in accordance with his strict code, was a changed man when dealing with his grandchildren. In fact, Elizabeth Logan wrote to her mother in 1878, "I am fearful of our visit next month, and wish you would speak seriously with Papa. He makes problems for us when he spoils the children, but he will listen to no one but you."

"Your father's regard for the children is so great," Georgy replied, "that I am unable to influence him. He likes to fool himself with the belief that he does not indulge them, and he is so stubborn that he will not be convinced otherwise."

Grandpa Porter was the greatest man in all the world to his grandchildren, officers and men of the Navy, and many other Americans. But large numbers of his fellow-countrymen began to regard him with suspicion in 1876, when the nation's press began to reveal the financial scandals that riddled the Grant Administration. Although the President himself was honest, his ignorance of politics and business had enabled numerous subordinates to line their own pockets. Virtually everyone in Washington was under a cloud, and Porter's expansive style of living caused eyebrows to be raised.

Secretary of the Navy Robeson was among those accused of accepting bribes from business interests in return for exerting his influence on their behalf, and a special Congressional committee began an investigation of his dealings with the builders of the Delaware-Chesapeake Canal. Porter was asked to testify, but was at home, ill. Newspapers hostile to the

Administration hinted rather broadly that they thought he was merely feigning sickness in order to protect himself. With his own good name in doubt, he dragged himself out of bed to appear before the committee.

As nearly as it is possible to judge from his correspondence and other evidence, Porter believed Robeson innocent of wrongdoing, and went before the committee determined to protect the secretary. But, in spite of the many years he had lived in Washington, the admiral was still as naive as he was blunt and honest, and was astonished when the anti-administration press, for political purposes, misconstrued his testimony as a frank indictment of Robeson.

The secretary's reputation was compromised, and he felt positive that Porter had attacked him with malicious intent. He made up his mind to retaliate. Accordingly, on August 10, 1876, he transferred the admiral from his post as uniformed head of the Navy to what was termed "waiting orders," meaning that Porter had no assignment of any kind. In addition to the loss of prestige, he suffered a salary cut from $13,000 to $8,000 a year.

Porter went straight to the President and laid the facts before him. General Sherman also hurried to the White House and conferred at length with Grant. The harried President was reluctant to engage in an open fight with a member of his Cabinet, and rather than intervene directly, simply changed Porter's orders to an "active" status. This restored his full salary, but did not return him to his previous post, which was comparable, in a later period, to that of Chief of Naval Operations.

In his new position, Porter had nothing to occupy him, and was so outraged he wanted to make all the facts in the case public. Always cooler in times of personal crisis, Sherman reminded him that the President would be dragged into the controversy. Grant was already suffering, and Sherman advised the admiral to say nothing, to sit at home and collect his salary and wait until the following March, when a newly-elected President would take office.

The advice was sound, and Porter accepted it. He found time hanging heavily on his hands, however, and finally turned to a project that had long been in his mind. He retired to the study on the top floor of the house on H Street. There, writing furiously, he produced a biography of his father, *Memoir of Commodore David Porter.*

The book was an immediate success, partly because of the author's renown, partly because of his energetic treatment of his subject. His approach was partisan, vehement, and aggressive; in his unalterable opinion, his father was one of the greatest of all Americans, and everyone who had ever opposed him was a villain or a fool. As always, Porter viewed life in terms of sharply defined blacks and whites.

The *Memoir*, although crude and overwritten, opened the door to a new, auxiliary career. Publishers and editors besieged the admiral, begging for more books. He was flattered, and in the next seven years happily wrote four novels, *Arthur Merton, The Adventures of Harry Marline, Robert Le Diable,* and *Allan Dare,* which was so long it had to be printed in two volumes. Aside from obviously autobiographical passages about the sea, these books were virtually without merit. Badly written and absurdly sentimental, their plots were ridiculous and their characters little more than caricatures. The author's name guaranteed their success, however, and *Allan Dare* was made into a play. Its opening night in New York was a memorable occasion, with Admiral Porter and General Sherman occupying a box.

Porter's career as an author inspired Sherman to write his autobiography, which made a fortune. This, in turn, caused Porter to think seriously about doing an autobiographical book of his own. His *Incidents and Anecdotes of the Civil War* was published in 1885, and was an overnight success.

It was unlike other books on the war and, though it dealt with factual material, was written with a surprisingly light hand, principally in anecdotal form. Porter agreed with Grant and General Robert E. Lee, whom he also admired, that the hatreds of the North and South should be forgotten and that both sections of the country should live and work together for the common good. The book not only reflected this view, but showed the author's deep sympathy for the South and her gallant fighting men who had persevered to the end against hopeless odds.

He was lavish in his praise of Admiral Farragut, and, of course, Generals Sherman and Grant. He also made plain his conviction that Abraham Lincoln had been the greatest of all Americans. But he treated Generals Butler, McClernand, and Banks with blunt scorn, and repeatedly emphasized his opinion that civilians who obtained commissions as generals because they had Presidential ambitions should be prevented by law from commanding troops in the field.

The better part of Porter's writing was done in his spare time. On March 4, 1877, the successful Republican candidate for President, Rutherford B. Hayes, took office. And one of his first acts was to return Admiral David D. Porter to his post as uniformed head of the Navy.

For the next fourteen years Porter worked incessantly to maintain and improve the Navy's standards. His insistence that there be no relaxation of discipline in peacetime caused professional seamen throughout the world to agree that the officers and men of the United States Navy were as efficient as those of the British Navy, which was universally regarded as the best. He continued to stress the need for accurate gunnery, repeatedly pointing out to subordinates that every major success the American Navy had enjoyed since its inception had been due, in the main, to the skill of its gunners. He simultaneously encouraged the development of new cannon, and badgered Congress for funds to procure weapons he believed would be effective.

"Porter's gunners," President Grover Cleveland said, in 1885, after spending a day at sea watching the admiral's nautical cannoneers blast target after target out of the water, "may be the most pampered elite corps on the high seas. I shall do all I can to treat them as Admiral Porter wishes them treated. They are accurate almost beyond credulity."

In the 1870's and 1880's, the United States was groping toward a new status as a world power. Conscious of the nation's growing prestige, Porter fought relentlessly for a Navy worthy of a great nation. He did not succeed, chiefly because the time was not ripe for such expansion. However, he made the American people conscious of the need, and the men who served under him provided the nucleus for the larger, more powerful Navy that came into existence on the eve of the Spanish-American War.

President Theodore Roosevelt, who served as Assistant Secretary of the Navy just prior to the outbreak of that war, and who ordered the construction of so many of the new vessels, paid tribute to Admiral Porter in 1906: "Our Navy," he said, "has become respected in every world capital and on every sea. We are capable of protecting ourselves against any foe. Our preparedness was achieved at a time when our people, wearied by the blood-letting of their terrible internal struggle, wanted peace and closed their eyes to the future, a future that their nation's growth had made inevitable. The keel of our new Navy was laid, almost singlehanded, by one man. Every American owes an eternal debt of gratitude to Admiral David Dixon Porter, a man of rare foresight, who had the courage to fight for what he knew was right."

Porter's struggle through the 1880's was wearying. In 1883 he celebrated his seventieth birthday, and his health, never good after the Civil War, began to fail. But it did not occur to him to retire. Following the example of Farragut, he remained on active duty. On the infrequent occasions when a Congressman or newspaper correspondent suggested that he spend the rest of his days at ease, he invariably replied, "An admiral of the Navy does not retire. He remains on active duty until he dies."

So it was Porter, expanding Farragut's theory, who was responsible for a policy established by Congress for both the Army and Navy after World War II. Five-star generals and admirals — new ranks established in that war — are never retired. No matter how they occupy themselves after leaving active service, they are still considered to be on duty.

Certainly no President or Secretary of the Navy thought of retiring Porter. Robeson was the last to make the attempt. Thereafter, each new administration "inherited" the uniformed head of the Navy. In fact, Porter's prestige throughout the United States was so great that no President would have dared to offend public opinion by ordering him to retire.

Aware of his unique, privileged status, the admiral did not hesitate to take full advantage of it on behalf of the principles he endorsed. In a typical, blunt public statement in 1880, he declared: "I am dismayed when I see how few boys from the South are enrolled in the regiment of midshipmen at the Naval

Academy. Many of our finest commodores and captains were Southern born and Southern bred. Surely the officers and men of the Confederate Navy proved their skill and courage. I, more than anyone now alive, can testify to their fighting qualities. The Navy is the Navy of all Americans, not merely of the states that formed the Union in the Civil War. Fifteen years have passed since that war ended, and it is time that the members of Congress representing the states of the South are granted their former privilege of appointing midshipmen to the Academy. The Navy and the country need those boys!"

The South rejoiced, and even men in the North who continued to bear grudges against their former enemies did not dare to oppose the admiral who had done so much for the Union cause. Both Houses of Congress promptly voted to restore to their Southern colleagues the right to appoint young men to the service academies.

But an editorial in the New York *Herald*, congratulating Porter on his "clever maneuver," infuriated him. "I am not clever," he said indignantly. "I wanted to see justice served, and I spoke the truth."

In spite of failing eyesight, repeated attacks of pleurisy, and other ailments, the admiral continued to drive himself at a pace that far younger men were incapable of tolerating. After the publication of his *Incidents and Anecdotes*, it occurred to him that he alone could write the authoritative history of the struggle at sea during the Civil War. The task would have occupied the full time of a competent historian for years, and most authors would have flinched at the prospect.

But the seventy-two-year-old David Dixon Porter felt certain he could write the book in his spare time, though the prospect alarmed his family. His son, Theodoric, sent him a letter urging him not to tax his health. This amused Porter. "In all modesty," he replied, "I am capable of writing more in three months than any ordinary writer would do in a year."

His estimate proved fairly accurate. *The Naval History of the Civil War*, which attempted to cover the entire four-year war at sea, required only four months of writing time. Most of the work was done at home, after dinner every evening, but he also made notes each day at his office as various pertinent thoughts occurred to him.

The book was far more a memoir than Porter intended it to be. Apparently he did not realize that his judgments were clouded by his feelings. Nor did it occur to him that his memory was less than perfect. The Navy's files were available to him, and he could have used them, had he wished, in order to prepare a book that would have been accurate in every detail. Instead, he elected to write the *Naval History* as he remembered the war.

Therefore, the actions in which he had played no part tended to be somewhat sketchy, and the accounts of his own operations were biased. He made a valiant effort to be fair, but even this approach led him into traps. His self-criticism was unsparing in his description of the failure of the Red River campaign, and his judgments were far too harsh. In addition, he was less than generous to the Army officers he still despised — Generals Butler and Banks.

The mere fact that the four-star admiral had written the *Naval History* made it a best seller, augmenting Porter's income, and allowing him to continue living in the style he enjoyed. Ben Butler, unable and unwilling to tolerate accusations of inefficiency, laziness, and even stupidity, replied in scathing statements to the press and in two bitter magazine articles which promptly aroused passions that, in theory, had been cooling for twenty-one years. Porter returned to the attack with his customary gusto, and the battle of words between the two old warriors was a major factor in making the *Naval History* the best-selling book of 1886.

In the years thereafter, Porter's health became increasingly fragile, but he paid no attention to the pleas of Georgy and his children to spare himself. When Government officials, Navy officers, and, finally, newspaper editorial writers added their voices to the clamor, he decided to make his position a matter of record.

"The Navy," he said in a public declaration, "is being badly neglected. Until she is given the ships, the men, and the armaments she needs to defend a growing nation in an era when other nations are busy building their fleets, I shall not rest. I would rather die at my desk than see the United States helpless and unprotected."

This statement, as he undoubtedly hoped and expected, helped change the Congressional climate, and in 1887 and 1888 the Navy was voted larger appropriations than otherwise would have been granted. Porter insisted that every penny be spent wisely, and, placing his trust in junior officers who had just returned to Washington from sea duty, listened to their advice and then lobbied effectively for the construction of the ships they thought would be the most effective in battle, should the United States become involved in a new war.

Most of the younger captains were enthusiastic supporters of the battleship, the logical successor, in the age of steam, to the old ships-of-the-line. Accordingly, Porter pushed hard for the construction of mammoth vessels, heavily armored, and carrying the most powerful guns afloat.

He neither sought nor listened to the advice of junior admirals, and on one occasion insulted his immediate subordinates by saying, "Admirals are old men, and want to use yesterday's weapons and techniques in fighting tomorrow's wars. Tomorrow's admirals — those who will take command in those wars — should be given a major voice in the determination of the ships and armor they will use."

As usual, his comments created a storm. Congressmen made speeches either supporting or denouncing him, and the newspapers again blazoned his name in their headlines. By now it had become apparent to the entire country that David Dixon Porter was incapable of living and working quietly. He claimed, in an interview with the New York *Herald*, that he did not deliberately seek headlines or controversy, but he admitted, with what was described as a rueful smile, that "I seem to have a knack for stirring up the mud at the bottom of the sea."

In the late winter of 1889, Porter made headlines of a different sort. On March 10th, he and Georgy celebrated their golden wedding anniversary, and gave a reception to commemorate the event. It was the last big party to be held at the house on H Street, and was one of the most memorable. Their children and grandchildren attended, of course, as did Senators, Congressmen, high Government officials, and many Army and Navy officers. Porter regretted — aloud — that men who had held high rank in the Confederate Navy and were living abroad could not attend.

President Benjamin Harrison made a point of paying his respects to the Porters. In a brief, gracious speech he told the guests that Porter and Georgy, as newlyweds, had attended the inauguration ball of his grandfather, President William Henry Harrison.

Georgy was asked to speak, but confined herself to a single, tart comment: "Everyone knows that my husband does all the talking for this family, and after fifty years we can't change our habits."

Porter, who disliked making formal speeches, was the last to address the guests. He was cheered when he said that Georgy was the loveliest of women. Warmed by the applause, he went on to discuss his other, equally intense love, the United States Navy, which he called the greatest in the world. Smiling at several British diplomats who were present, he added, "You think me boastful, gentlemen, but the day is not far distant when our Navy shall surpass the ruler of the seas." Only the most optimistic of his vehemently patriotic fellow countrymen were able to take this prediction seriously.

Finally, ignoring his own ailments, he said, "As for me, I'm still a young man. If I'm not young in years, I'm still young enough in spirit to fight one more war, should the occasion arise."

President Harrison, watched closely by members of the diplomatic corps, applauded politely, hoping to indicate that he wasn't thinking of making war on any nation. The other American guests were less restrained, and roared their approval before everyone adjourned to the dining room and auxiliary parlors for a champagne supper.

Newspapers throughout the United States called the party the most important social event of the year, and a less heroic figure might have retired from public life. But Porter continued to make news. The occasion was his appointment to temporary command of the Navy's combined fleets, which had gathered in New York harbor for the one hundredth anniversary of George Washington's inauguration as the country's first President.

From April 30th through May 2nd, Porter put the many warships through intricate maneuvers, the press using the event to print laudatory reviews of his long career. It was impossible for his past to be discussed in print without mentioning his personal foes, and Ben Butler received the brunt of criticism as old memories were revived. New Orleans newspapers resurrected the story — which may have been a canard — that Butler had stolen the silver spoons from the St. Charles Hotel when he hurriedly departed from the city. The South was still suffering from the harsh injustices of Reconstruction, and the tale was reprinted everywhere in the area. Meanwhile, the Northern newspapers were busily recalling Butler's failure during the first attack on Fort Fisher.

Butler, seventy-one years old and living in retirement in Washington, was startled and angered by the sudden notoriety. His advancing years had not taught him caution, and in trying to divert attention from himself he made the absurd charge that Admiral Porter had fled from the Confederate forts below New Orleans.

Had Porter been younger he would have laughed off the claim that he had been a coward. However, he was also growing old, and furiously demanded that Butler produce proof. This the former general could not do. Instead, he published a pamphlet at his own expense, in which — quoting excerpts from David's *Incidents and Anecdotes* — he tried to substantiate his assertion.

Porter's family and friends could not silence him, and he angrily told the press, "Butler is a fool."

Proud of his intellect, Butler lashed back, and the two old men engaged in a heated session of undignified name-calling. Only Georgy, among all his friends and relatives, was able to finally intervene and silence Porter, thus bringing the meaningless feud to a close. By this time, however, the damage had been done, and people too young to remember the admiral's great exploits were disgusted. His reputation suffered a blow from which it did not recover for many decades, his fellow citizens failing to realize that he was becoming senile.

In the summer of 1890, while enjoying a holiday at Newport, Porter stubbornly ignored the advice of his physicians and took a long, brisk walk on a very warm day. He suffered a heart attack that was almost fatal, and though he recovered sufficiently to leave his bed, both mind and body were impaired. When he returned to Washington in the early autumn, his friends there were distressed to discover that he sometimes rambled incoherently.

On the morning of February 13, 1891, Porter succumbed to another heart attack. Several of his children were with him at the time, but Georgy, herself ill, was asleep in another room.

On February 15th, Washington gave the great admiral one of the most impressive funerals in the city's history. President Harrison led the official mourners, and thousands of Marines and sailors marched in the procession. During a lucid moment in the preceding months, Porter had revised his will, and had named his own pallbearers. All but one were rear admirals who had served under him during his long career. The exception was General Joseph E. Johnston of the Confederate Army, one of the South's most gallant heroes, whose presence signified Porter's desire to reunite the North and South in peace for all time.

Overshadowed through much of his lifetime by Admiral Farragut, and by the appearance only a few years after his death of a new luminary, Admiral George Dewey, David Dixon Porter has not emerged until the present day — almost a century later — in true perspective as one of America's most influential and courageous sailors, an admiral worthy of the exalted station he achieved.

A Note to the Reader

If you have enjoyed this book enough to leave a review on **Amazon** and **Goodreads**, then we would be truly grateful.

The Estate of Noel B. Gerson

Sapere Books is an exciting new publisher of brilliant fiction and popular history.

To find out more about our latest releases and our monthly bargain books visit our website:
saperebooks.com